YOUR LIGHT
GIVES US HOPE

24 Daily Practices for Advent

YOUR LIGHT GIVES US HOPE

24 Daily Practices for Advent

ANSELM GRÜN

Translated by Mark S. Burrows

PARACLETE PRESS
BREWSTER, MASSACHUSETTS

2017 First Printing

Your Light Gives Us Hope: 24 Daily Practices for Advent

Original title: Dein Licht schenkt uns Hoffnung. 24 Rituale für den Advent by Anselm Grün
© 2015 by Vier-Türme GmbH Verlag, Münsterschwarzach (Germany)

English translation Copyright © 2017 by Mark S. Burrows
All rights reserved.

ISBN 978-1-61261-904-0

Library of Congress Cataloging-in-Publication Data is available

Names: Grèun, Anselm, author.
Title: Your light gives us hope : twenty-four daily practices for Advent / by
    Anselm Grèun ; translated by Mark S. Burrows.
Other titles: Dein Licht schenkt uns Hoffnung. English
Description: Brewster, Massachusetts : Paraclete Press Inc., 2017.
Identifiers: LCCN 2017020889 | ISBN 9781612619040 (pbk.)
Subjects: LCSH: Advent—Meditations.
Classification: LCC BV40 .G77913 2017 | DDC 242/.332—dc23
LC record available at https://lccn.loc.gov/2017020889

10 9 8 7 6 5 4 3 2 1

Published by Paraclete Press
Brewster, Massachusetts
www.paracletepress.com

Printed in the United States of America

CONTENTS

Translator's Foreword, by Mark S. Burrows   vii

INTRODUCTION: *Advent, the Season*   xiii
of Arrival

I: THE FIRST SUNDAY OF ADVENT: 1
Come, Lord Jesus!
  1 December LIGHT   4
  2 December WAITING   6
  3 December WATCHING   8
  4 December YEARNING   10
  5 December ARRIVING   12
  6 December SAINT NICHOLAS DAY   14

II: THE SECOND SUNDAY OF ADVENT: 17
Prepare the Way of the Lord!
  7 December THINKING ANEW   20
  8 December MARY IMMACULATE   22
  9 December FORGIVENESS   25
  10 December PREPARE THE WAY   28
  11 December MOVING MOUNTAINS   30
  12 December CLEANSING   32
  13 December TWO BEARERS OF LIGHT: 34
    ST. ODILIA AND ST. LUCY

III: The Third Sunday of Advent: 37

Rejoice!

14 December GOOD DEEDS   42

15 December JOY   44

16 December THE LORD IS NEAR   46

17 December SEEKING A PLACE OF   48
    REFUGE

18 December ANGELS   50

19 December THE STUMP   53

20 December SWORDS TO PLOWSHARES   55

IV: The Fourth Sunday of Advent: 57

*Let It Be with Me According
to Your Word!*

21 December MARY, THE EXAMPLE OF   62
    FAITH

22 December GOD'S BIRTH IN OUR SOUL   64

23 December ENCOUNTER   67

24 December CELEBRATING A NEW   69
    BEGINNING

Afterword   73

TRANSLATOR'S
FOREWORD

Fr. Anselm Grün needs little introduction in Germany. He is well-known as a best-selling author of books on Christian faith and spirituality, which together have sold more than 14 million copies, and regularly gives talks and workshops across the country as well as appearing frequently on television. He does all this while living out his vow of "stability of place" at the Benedictine abbey of Münsterschwarzach, not far from the city of Würzburg in Lower Franconia. There, he joins his brothers in what St. Benedict described in his *Rule* as "a school for the Lord's service," which in this case is a large community of monks with a strong local ministry and a global vision of mission.

Within this community, which he joined as a nineteen-year-old in the early 1960s, Fr. Grün joins his brothers in the commitment to "work and pray," as the motto of the Benedictine order puts it. For more than thirty years, he held the important position St. Benedict called the "cellarer," the monk charged with managing the provisions of the monastery and thus responsible, as the *Rule* puts it, "for everything"—a kind of CFO for the abbey's business operations. In this role, he had oversight of a workforce employing more than three hundred people in some twenty departments, hardly what we think of when we imagine a monk observing the rule of silence.

Yet while his work as cellarer surely grounded him in the often stressful realities of modern business, the wisdom he brings in his writings has more to do with St. Benedict's daring conviction that "the divine presence is everywhere"—in our work and in our prayer, in the monastery as in "the world." Readers will come to recognize the impact of this belief throughout the pages that follow.

All this suggests why, in reading Fr. Grün, one does not encounter the voice of a reclusive monk. His God is not hiding somewhere in the monastery, out of reach of ordinary folks. On the contrary, and in keeping with the Advent tidings, he discovers God in the scriptural promises that point to the One who comes among us, the incarnate Lord in Jesus of Nazareth. At the heart of this season, we come face-to-face—quite literally—with the God who takes up human life and lives as one with us. This is the Messiah announced in Advent as Emmanuel, the God-with-us who was born in a simple manger in Bethlehem. And it is this God who seeks to be present "everywhere" among us in our lives today.

This day-by-day devotional guide to Advent appeared in the original German edition in 2015 and quickly became a well-loved companion for thousands of readers: Roman Catholic and Protestant, doubters and seekers. They found here what they have come to expect from Fr. Grün's wide-ranging writings: namely, nourishment for their spiritual hunger and illumination for their path in life. It is a privilege to bring this devotional gem to English readers.

What you will find in these pages, meant to be read and pondered day by day during the weeks leading up to Christmas, is a message shaped by a dialogue between theology and psychology, faith and spirituality, divine revelation and human experience. Throughout the short chapters here, Fr. Grün meets us in our longing for wholeness, the desire that marks Advent as the "overture" to the larger symphony of the church's year. These daily readings offer a centering path through these often hectic weeks, reminding us, as the opening words of the *Rule* put it, to learn to "listen . . . with the ears of [our] heart."

How do we learn to do this? Here, a few words of introduction might help orient you to this "guidebook" and the wisdom it reveals.

First, *Advent is a season of rebirth*. Fr. Grün reminds us that Advent is not simply a backward-looking celebration of ancient history, but rather a period of spiritual preparation when we ready ourselves for Christ's birth *in us*. This theme, above all others, shapes the pages of this devotional book, drawing on ancient prophecies and later church traditions to suggest how this season proclaims the coming of God in our lives, here and now. Not accidentally, this season marks the beginning of the church's year, which starts not with the first of January but with the four Sundays leading up to Christmas. Thus the author reminds us that Advent celebrates the story of the Incarnation as a "new beginning," not simply in a manger long ago and far away, but in the realities of our daily lives. God longs to be born among us in our world—and in your life.

Second, *Advent is a season of renewal*. It is an opportunity to give ourselves to the work of uncluttering our lives, a time when we learn to open ourselves to the renewing gift of grace. In this season, we find ourselves called to "begin again" with the gospel, which promises light in the darkness, the light that brings us hope against the tides of despair. It is the season when we celebrate the birth of new life, *our* new life, in the midst of what we experience of disappointment and death.

Third, *Advent is a season of arrival*. This season invites us to celebrate God's coming in the ordinary realities of our lives. Daily readings take their point of departure from scriptural texts, the occasion of particular saints' days, and Advent traditions, all inviting us to make progress in our journey into the life of God. Alongside readings for the first twenty-four days of December are longer chapters devoted to each of the four Sundays, suggesting how the themes of these weeks shape an overarching narrative pattern of "arrival" for Advent. Readers steeped in the church's practices as well as those less familiar with them will find this book a helpful guide into the theological, spiritual, and psychological meaning unveiled to us in this season. Advent is about God's arrival in our lives, accompanied as we are by unexpected messengers and invited to "prepare the way" in our lives for his coming.

How might you use this book? The simplest way would be to begin with the first Sunday in Advent, reading the short introductory chapter and then setting aside time each morning to read the short chapter for each day. One might also begin at the end, with the author's afterword, for it is here that Fr. Grün gathers the themes explored throughout this book in a useful overview. The "Sunday" chapters might also be read each week at home, around the dinner table, or with a church group. But none of this is necessary; the short entries devoted to each of the twenty-four days leading up to Christmas are sufficient in themselves.

Whether used by individuals or with families or parish groups, this book hopes to deepen our *experience* of God during Advent, and that means coming to know ourselves for who we truly are. The encouragement and challenge Fr. Grün shares with us here has much to do with the utterly human focus of the story: the birth of a child born in difficult circumstances far from the comforts of home, and the family's hasty departure as migrants in search of safety from threat of death. In this case, they sought refuge in Egypt, a land Israel had long remembered as a place of slavery; it was there that the holy family found protection, against all expectations.

Rarely has this story seemed as poignant as it does now, particularly in Europe, where a refugee crisis has led millions of displaced persons to flee their homelands in the Middle East and North Africa because of the threat of war, religious persecution, or hunger. Fr. Grün reminds us that the gospel stories face such struggles head-on: a vulnerable infant, born out of wedlock to Jewish parents, becomes with his parents a refugee, seeking safety from the threat of death and finding welcome in a strange and forbidding land.

Fr. Grün presents this ancient story as it has come to be embellished over the centuries with vivid traditions in the church's life. He guides us, as an author widely recognized for a wisdom at once spiritual and practical to the inner riches of our Advent faith. In these pages, through the days of this season, you will find yourself called like the shepherds, and lured like the Magi, to receive the gift of God's birth, in the "manger" of your heart. This is a book written to nourish your hunger for love and meet the longings of your heart. May you here find yourself welcomed ever more deeply into the mystery of the God who, as Fr. Grün reminds us, "desires this day to begin anew with you," for this God is "the one who is always eternally new"—"everywhere" in this world, as Benedict claimed, and in the daily realities of our lives.

Mark S. Burrows
Bochum, Germany

INTRODUCTION

Advent, the Season of Arrival

A dvent is the quiet season when we wait for Jesus's coming. For the word *Advent* simply means "arrival." We wait for Jesus's arrival in our heart. But we also wait for his coming at the end of the ages. Over the ages Christians have celebrated this season as a special time of preparation leading to the celebration of Christmas, one marked by many family observances. It is a season when we draw on traditions and rituals that usher us into the mystery of Christmas, not simply in the church but in our daily lives. In such ways, we come to discover the theological truth of this season in intimate ways that stir our hearts.

In this book, I hope to introduce the most important message of Advent through brief, daily meditations that explore some particular aspect of this message, together with a practice inviting you to deepen your experience of its meaning in your daily life.

You will also find here short chapters introducing the message central to each of the four Advent Sundays. The first of these Sundays focuses on apocalyptic passages from the Scriptures that tell of the end times and warn us to be watchful. The second and third Sundays place John the Baptist at the center of the story, the voice "crying in the wilderness," calling us to repent and await the coming Messiah. The fourth and final Sunday focuses on Mary, who is to give birth to the promised Savior. She embodies the true meaning of Advent, directing us toward Christ, who is coming *to us* and also desires to be born *in us*. For this reason, I have included a meditation for each of these Sundays, alongside one for each of the days in December leading up to Christmas. My intention throughout is to offer these reflections in order that the mystery of Advent might illumine our daily lives as well as those of our families and church communities.

It has long been customary in Germany, as in the United States, to hang up an Advent calendar at home during this season, with windows for each of the twenty-four days preceding Christmas. In earlier times, each concealed an Advent symbol, image, or Bible verse; today, though, these calendars seem intended mostly for children, with each window holding a piece of candy, chocolate, or a small toy. In this book, each day will offer a short reflection together with a simple practice designed to be used either singly or with one's family or friends. For example, on the Saturday evening before the start of each new week during Advent, one might read the short biblical text that precedes each of these meditations, using this theme to shape one's path through the coming week. Alongside these four entries is one for each of the days leading up to Christmas, offering a meditation on a particular theme and related practice to shape the day ahead. When we choose to give shape to Advent in such deliberate ways, we will find this season to be a time of blessing for us and for our families. In so doing, we learn to welcome this season as a time when we await Christ's coming in our lives, thereby coming to experience Advent in a new way.

Today, the season of Advent has become a premature celebration of Christmas. As with the Christmas markets found in cities and towns all across Germany, department stores begin broadcasting

Christmas carols in early November, weeks before Advent has even begun. This pushing forward of Christmas prevents us from experiencing the mystery of Advent as it should be celebrated. One of my intentions here is to recover the original meaning of this season as a time of stillness, waiting, and watching in order to experience more intentionally its saving power in our lives.

Yours,
Fr. Anselm Grün, OSB

I

THE FIRST SUNDAY
OF ADVENT

Come, Lord Jesus!

Each of the first three Gospels—Matthew, Mark, and Luke—include Jesus's teachings about the end of time, and one of these passages is traditionally read on the first Sunday of Advent. Such readings about the "apocalypse" might well be difficult for us as modern people, but the root of the word simply means "to discover," or "unveil." These texts seek to show us what's what in our world, reminding us that this world is not eternal. It is not our ultimate home. We yearn for another world, one shaped by God and not by the powers of this age. This is the reason the church reminds us of this theme today, honoring our yearning for God's world and our longing for Christ's coming at the beginning of Advent. When Jesus comes again, this world as we know it will be transformed.

Of course, Jesus desires to come to each of us in every moment of our lives. Indeed, the parable of the gatekeeper, recounted in Mark's Gospel, reminds us of his continual coming among us. We, too, should be like the gatekeeper who waits for the coming of his Lord, refusing to allow any strangers into the house but waiting patiently to open his door for the Lord. Evagrius of Pontus, a monk of the fourth century ce, describes our proper posture through this image of the gatekeeper. We should guard the doors of our hearts, as this gatekeeper had done, keeping an eye on this inner door so that no strange thoughts or emotions might enter. For we are often not lords of our own house, which all too often seems filled with other occupants—injuries that hurt us, annoyances that root themselves in us, fears and disappointments that dwell in us. We should ask of every thought that seeks entry into our hearts this question: *Who are you? And what do you want with me? Do you have some important message for me, or are you simply an undesirable stranger who wants to claim me for his own purposes?* Only in such a way can we discern what to let in, and what to keep out. We should keep watch over the door of our heart so that we are truly present when the Lord himself comes to us and asks to enter. This, then, is the goal of our watching: to be ready to receive the Lord, who stands at the door of our heart and knocks, asking to come in.

Of course, we know that the Lord, who is "everywhere" as St. Benedict reminds us, is already present in our lives. But because we are often not paying proper attention, and too often seem to be absent from the house of our own heart, we experience the Lord as the one who is coming. In Advent, we await Christ's coming, and hope for his entrance into our heart. Thus the call of longing— "Come, Lord Jesus"—that so shaped the earliest Christians is the call to come home to our true self, which means to come home to our own heart. Only when we are truly present to ourselves can the Lord come to us and enter our lives. Thus Advent is a season in which we hope to awake from our sleep, and so come to see what is truly real in our lives. Advent is a season meant to prepare us for the Lord's coming so that we might be at home when he knocks at our heart's door. And he comes to us every day, and in so many ways: in our brothers and sisters as in the stillness when the clamor of our noisy thoughts finally abates. He knocks on our door through the quiet impulses of our heart. When we open to him, Advent comes to fulfillment in us, because when the Lord comes to us, the one whom we long for enters into the house of our heart, coming into us as the King of Glory.

When the Gospel speaks of the end of the world, we don't need to worry about *when* this world might end. For each of us, the world ceases to exist at the time of our death. The end of the world arrives for each of us at *our* ending, and then it is that the kingdom of God breaks upon us. At that time God will come to change us entirely. Thus Advent is the time when we become aware of the temporality of our life. The thought of our death, when the world as we know it comes to an end for us, is ultimately an invitation—to live with purpose and come to sense the mystery of our life in every moment. Precisely because our life is finite, we are challenged to become aware of the present moment and consider what path we want to pursue in this world.

1 December
LIGHT

DURING ADVENT we hear marvelous texts that come to us from the prophet Isaiah. Often these speak of the light that breaks into the darkness. The composer Georg Friedrich Handel set to music the beginning of the ninth chapter of Isaiah in a wonderful bass aria that reads:

> *The people that walked in darkness have seen a great light;*
> *and they that dwell in the land of the shadow of death,*
> *upon them hath the light shined. (Isa. 9:2 KJV)*

The light that is coming into our world in Jesus wants to bring light into our darkness. Who are those who dwell in the land of darkness? Those whose hearts are dark and sorrowful. But when the light of God shines into this darkness, everything becomes light in our lives and we find our mood brightening. Advent is a season in which we find ourselves invited to face our darkness and bring it to the light of Christ so that his light might shine within us.

☙ Practice

Light a candle in a dark room in your house and sit comfortably and quietly in front of it. Watch to see how the flickering light brightens everything in the room, casting a soft light upon it all. In your mind consider how Christ, at Christmas, shines his tender light into every room within your heart—illumining your fears and your restlessness, your superficiality and your anger, your jealousy.

Close your eyes and see, with your inner eye, how the light of this candle shines upon you: on your body, your chest and heart, your neck, your hands, your legs and feet, and all the way to your toes. Now allow this light to find those places in your life that are dark and in greatest need of it.

This is the light that wants to shine in your home, in the places where you work and sleep. But also in those places where you are worried and troubled. In the times when you gather with your family and friends. And in all the conflicts and tensions you face with others.

Trust this light, which sometimes seems dim to you, to shine brightly upon every aspect of your life, bringing the mystery of God's love into your heart and home. In this way, you will begin to discover that you can be truly at home wherever you are. For we can only dwell in the "house of our heart" where this mystery dwells. Here we find our true home, and here we learn to welcome God who seeks to come to us as light and love. Only then do we find ourselves truly at home, even in the midst of what is restless within us.

2 *December*
WAITING

WAITING IS a fundamental part of our lives. We often find ourselves waiting. We all know what it is like to wait for someone we expect to come, often becoming quite impatient until they finally arrive. Or we find ourselves waiting for a call and looking at our watches as we hope to hear the phone ring; after all, we'd agreed on a time to talk. And we often find ourselves waiting in lines at a store, a bus stop, or in airport security lines that stand between us and making our flight on time. Waiting shapes much of our lives. And, to be honest, we often find it hard to wait, especially in circumstances over which we have little control.

Advent is a time of waiting, a season of expectation when we learn how to wait for God's coming into our hearts—again and again. In these weeks, we know in our hearts that when God does come all will be well and we will experience what it means to come home to ourselves. We have just this experience when we give ourselves to those longings of our heart that reach beyond this world, and when we come to see that, we do have the strength to wait. For it is in this waiting that we come to know our true self; in this experience, we feel ourselves becoming one in the moment. We discover a quiet center within ourselves, and realize that this moment holds everything that is important for us. We are simply here, now, in this moment—aware, attentive, and present.

❧ Practice

Pay particular attention, throughout the day, to times when you find yourself waiting—for an elevator, for a bus or subway, in a line at the store, in traffic congestion, for a guest to arrive.

In such moments, pay attention to what it means to wait—with *expectation*. Attend to your impatience, saying quietly to yourself: *It really is not that important when I arrive.* Give yourself fully to this moment, and seek to rest within yourself. Say to yourself: *"I'm not just waiting for the bus; I'm waiting for God, who is already present in my life. I'm waiting for the Lord who wants me to welcome him, and who will come when I am truly present."*

If you sense your own impatience, give it to God. When you do this, you'll find yourself becoming quiet in your heart and begin to sense God protecting you. You'll start to feel yourself becoming free of the pressure of fulfilling others' expectations. In this moment, give your waiting and even your impatience to God. In doing so, you'll begin to find your discomfort fade away. A newfound patience will bring new energy and aliveness to you.

December 3
WATCHING

ADVENT IS a time of attentiveness, vigilance, and mindfulness. Theologians writing during the early centuries of Christianity often interpreted the human condition as one of drowsiness. They knew that we are easily lulled to sleep by the illusions we hold about our lives. We want to live with greater intentionality, but in actuality find our spirits becoming dulled by the onslaught of images that the media besiege us with. During Advent, we even find ourselves becoming deaf to the Christmas carols constantly playing in stores and malls. All this can create an unreal atmosphere that immerses us in a make-believe world.

Our task is to awaken ourselves from the stupor of this world of appearances. Indeed, the Jesuit writer Anthony de Mello defines "mysticism" in these terms: it is an awakening to what is truly real. I must wake up so that I can begin to see reality for what it truly is.

❧ Practice

One form of watching is mindfulness. Decide to approach this day with a mindful heart. When you wake, pay attention to the fact that this is a new day, one in which God invites you into his presence. When you shower, pay attention to what you are doing: as you wash, savor the experience of cleansing yourself of what is unclean, both on the outside and within. When you sit down to breakfast, pay attention to what you are eating. Slow down. Savor each bite.

When you leave your home, be mindful of the people you'll meet. Try to be present to each one. Be mindful of the steps you take. Be aware of the fact that you are not simply going from one place to another. Your outer progress is a reflection of what it means to be on an *inner* journey, one you did not determine. For your life is an ongoing journey bringing change in your life.

Be mindful of what you begin this day. And pay attention to what will come to an end. Give up imagining that you have finished with this or that, so that you might become mindful of what still awaits you. Be aware that God's blessing rests within each moment like a protective mantle. With such mindfulness, you'll find yourself walking differently as you go.

December 4
YEARNING

ADVENT IS a time in which we become more aware of our yearning—for a sense of home and security, for love and happiness.

While every season of the church's year is a time of healing, Advent is the season when our addictions should be transformed into healthy forms of longing. For addictions are forms of suppressed yearning, which properly speaking are meant to lead us beyond what is finite and earthly. For no person, no character trait, no success can ever satisfy our deepest desires. These can only be fulfilled by God. That's why our true yearning carries us through and beyond the things of our daily lives, and finally into God's presence.

Such desire, as poets often remind us, constitutes our true worth as human beings. The writer Marcel Proust put it this way: "Yearning helps bring things to bloom." In reality, desires are traces God has rooted deeply in our heart. Many complain, of course, that they can't sense God's presence, and it's true that we can't always experience God directly. But we can become more aware each day of the traces of God in our hearts. And our longing for God is already a sign of his presence, just as love is already present in our yearning for love.

Today, the fourth of December, is the Feast of St. Barbara. Following an old European tradition for this saint's day, we cut and place what we call "St. Barbara Branches"—these are generally branches from cherry trees—into vases of water, watching through the days of Advent as they begin to show signs of budding until they blossom on or around Christmas. These branches are like the signs of love we carry within us, which even in this cold season want to blossom and fill our hearts with joy.

Such St. Barbara Branches are an expression of our longing for love and for a sense of comfort, a yearning for warmth and tenderness in the midst of such wintry times. If possible, cut several branches from a flowering fruit tree near your house, and put them in a vase of fresh water in your home. Imagine how they will eventually begin to grow from the small buds, finally blossoming at Christmastime.

❧ Practice

Sit before a burning candle, perhaps with the vase of cut branches nearby, and place your hands at the center of your chest. Your hands will feel a warmth here, and this gesture evokes the sense of yearning you carry in your heart. Think about what it is you long for—for love, for happiness, for peace, for stillness, for God.

Think about how love is present to you within this longing, even here and now. You need not feel unhappy about someone who has not returned your love. In your yearning for love you already sense the love that no one can take from you.

Carry this yearning into your daily life. You will discover that when God meets this yearning, you no longer need to depend on anything or anyone to satisfy your desires—in your workplace, in your family, or in other relationships. Simply become grateful in the ways you enjoy your life for what it is. Indeed, experiences of fulfillment and disappointment, of success and failure, are what keep this sense of longing alert. Within *this* yearning, begin to feel a measure of the deep inner peace that nothing can take away.

December 5
ARRIVING

WE WAIT during Advent for the coming of Jesus in our lives. In German, we have several variations for the word *arriving*. One of these is the word *Ankommen*. When we go on vacation, we often feel—especially on the very first day—that we've not properly "arrived." We find ourselves still thinking about work. Or problems at home still occupy our thoughts.

And we often have the sense that we've not yet arrived at our true self. That we haven't yet come home to who we truly are. That we're living outside ourselves. We find ourselves caught in a hamster wheel, feeling as if we're always on the move but never coming to our real self—and so never fully "arrive" at all.

Advent invites us to come home to ourselves. In Jesus's parable of the prodigal son, some translations speak of the moment when the prodigal son "came to his senses" (Lk. 15:17), though the Greek literally speaks of when he "came to himself." Having squandered his inheritance, the prodigal son threw himself into a life devoted to external things. But when he finally "came to himself," when he "arrived" at his true self, he came to see the mistakes he'd made in letting his lower desires control him.

Advent is the season when we find ourselves invited to come home to who we truly are. When we do, we come to sense the second meaning of the prodigal son's experience of arriving—that is, when he discovered his true identity. Only when we come home to who we truly are do we begin to discover how we can get along better with others. In this way, we find ourselves accepted by them, for they can sense when we are present to our true self. When this is not the case, we fail in our attempts to find acceptance from others; in such cases, our encounters with them remain superficial at best.

℁ Practice

Take time for a long walk sometime today. Once you have walked for a bit, look for a place where you can pause and be still for a little while. Find a place to sit, or stand quietly, asking yourself this: *"Have I truly come home to the person I am? Have I 'arrived'? Am I just here in this place? Or am I truly here, in my real self, in this particular place where I find myself now?"*

Imagine coming home, like the prodigal son, to your true self. Think about how you have come to this place and time, through all the commotion of your daily life, in order to arrive at who you really are. Take a moment to sense what this is like, in the quiet of your heart. Savor what it feels like to be present to yourself. Then imagine Jesus coming to meet you here and now, like the father who came out to embrace his lost son, because like him you are now present to your true self. Open your heart so that Jesus can come into you and welcome you in this moment.

December 6
SAINT NICHOLAS DAY

TODAY IS the Feast of St. Nicholas, a bishop who lived in the city of Myra (in present-day Turkey) in the fourth century CE. He is surely among the most beloved of all the saints. Many traditions surround this good man, most of them focusing on children. The legends about him describe the remarkable kindness he showed toward others, especially those in need—and above all children.

I have an icon of St. Nicholas in my room that portrays him as a person of immeasurable love. I cannot look at this image without feeling drawn to be filled with the same love Nicholas had and shared with others. One could say that this saint didn't simply love individuals; he embodied love itself. His very being was grounded in the desire to enable this love to flow out into the world.

A well-known story about St. Nicholas relates his encounter with a nobleman, a rich man who'd fallen on hard times and lost his wealth. In despair, and to avoid starvation, he gave his three daughters over to a life of prostitution. Now when Nicholas heard of this, he came to the distraught man's house—not once, but on three successive nights, each time throwing a larger sum of money into the house in order to save each of the daughters from this fate. On the third night, the man decided to stay awake in order to see who his generous benefactor was. He immediately recognized the good bishop and fell to his knees in gratitude, but Nicholas ordered him to stand and promise not to say a word about this to anyone.

You see, Nicholas wanted to do such good works secretly. His desire was to lead others to God as a loving father figure, like our heavenly Father who cares for us. And he did this not with a mother's tender love, but with the strength of a father's love, which is able to free and protect us.

Such a father's love calls us to live beyond ourselves and leads us to the very source of life. It is an appropriate reminder of the life and witness of St. Nicholas, then, that on this day we celebrate his coming to children, showing them how to live generously by showering them with a father's gifts. What a marvelous tradition that on this day, in Germany, we give gifts to children to sweeten their lives so that they might experience a measure of the sweetness of God's fatherly love for us.

℈ Practice

In a quiet moment, think about your own father. What has he given you? What does he mean for you? How does he support you? Can you turn to him with all your worries and troubles? Can you rely on him? Surely he gave you gifts. But he also had his limits, and couldn't fulfill all the expectations you might have had for him as a father.

Now, imagine God as the Father who fulfills all the yearnings we associate with fatherhood. He accepts us unconditionally. He supports us to the point that we dare to take responsibility for our lives. Think of those who've shared with you some portion of God's fatherly presence. Thank God that he has sent you such persons who, like St. Nicholas, showed you the strength of a father's love. Give thanks for the ways they've encouraged you to affirm that, yes, it is good that you're alive. And, on the strength of this sense of goodness, dare to live your life!

If you're a father yourself, pay special attention today to the many ways you might support your children. Take time to share with them encouraging words. Embrace them and tell them this: *"It's a gift that you're alive! I'm here for you! I'm behind you, no matter what happens along the way!"*

II

THE SECOND SUNDAY OF ADVENT

Prepare the Way of the Lord!

On the second Sunday in Advent, John the Baptist's preaching assumes a central position in the way he points to the Messiah's coming. In each of the first three Gospels, we hear him quote the prophet Isaiah:

> *The voice of one calling out in the wilderness:*
> *Prepare the way of the Lord,*
> *make his paths straight! (Lk. 3:4; Matt. 3:3; Mk. 1:3)*

John the Baptist came preaching a message of conversion, or *metanoia* in the Greek, which means a "transforming of the mind." He called those who came out to hear him at the Jordan to change their lives, for the kingdom of heaven was near. What does such a transformation mean? It means learning to think differently, daring to consider things from a new standpoint, seeing as God sees and not based on our own needs. If we can learn to engage reality from God's vantage point, we'll find ourselves encouraged to behave differently. We'll begin to learn how to avoid wrong paths in our lives, and find and follow the way that leads to life.

Advent calls us to think about the paths we've followed in the past year, and change directions if these have led us down wrong paths.

Of course, John the Baptist wasn't simply a prophet who preached conversion of life. He also prophesied the coming of salvation. In Luke's Gospel, we hear him proclaim this message again with a reference from Isaiah:

All flesh shall see the salvation of God. (Lk. 3:6; see Isa. 40:5)

In both Matthew and Mark's Gospels, John the Baptist points directly to the Messiah:

One who is more powerful than I is coming; I am not worthy to untie the thong of his sandals. (Lk. 3:16)

He refused to speak of himself, but pointed rather to the coming of the Messiah. He retreated behind his message as a forerunner whose preaching announced the Lord's coming.

This is a wonderful image for us as well, for here we might truly see ourselves as persons also called to announce God's coming. We, too, are to go "ahead of the Lord," so that he might come to others through us. We, too, are called to encounter others in a way that awakens their yearning "to wait for another," to hope for the coming of the one who meets our deepest longings. With John the Baptist we, too, are witnesses to Christ, called to point to him with our entire being. The question is whether others can see and recognize this witness, because often enough the testimony we render in our lives points to our own brokenness, untrustworthiness, superficiality, or fear.

What is it that others see in our lives? How might they come to recognize Christ in us? Are we content with ourselves, resigned to our life as it is, or does our life point beyond itself to the One in whom we find our very being, the One who alone can fulfill our deepest yearning?

John the Baptist calls us to bear witness to Christ with our entire lives, and thus to retreat behind our works, behind our words, such that we no longer stand in the foreground but rather allow Christ to shine forth in us.

December 7
THINKING ANEW

JOHN THE BAPTIST came preaching "conversion of life" (*metanoia*), calling those who journeyed out to meet him to a life shaped by radical rethinking, by a different kind of thinking. We should no longer emulate this world in the ways we think. We should look beyond our lives, and finally beyond this world, in order to discover how God thinks about things. This calls us to an altogether new way of thinking, one the apostle Paul gives voice to in his letter to the Christians in Rome:

> *Do not be conformed to this world, but be transformed by the renewing of your minds, so that you may discern what is the will of God—what is good and acceptable and perfect. (Rom. 12:2)*

Of course, a true "conversion of mind" doesn't simply mean rethinking, or thinking in a new way. It goes further, calling us to look *behind* things for the deepest source of reality. Such a conversion also means not getting stuck thinking about what others have thought, but rather trusting our own thinking when it calls us to step out of the mainstream. It calls us to think and act in ways congruent with our true understanding, and in sync with the deep desires of our heart. That is, it calls us to think with our heart and not only with our head.

ஃ Practice

Sit down comfortably in a chair and think about what is stirring within you. What are you thinking about in your own life? What are your thoughts about others? And then ask yourself this: *"Are these thoughts really true? Or are they judgments I've made on the basis of my own narrowness of mind or sensitivities?"*

Now, imagine this: *"What does God think of me? Who am I in God's presence? What does God think of my life? Is my life authentic? Am I true to my real self? What does God think of those with whom I live my life? What does God think of those with whom I have difficulties, those I don't like?"*

Take a moment and wish for such persons a measure of God's blessing. See if you notice that offering this blessing has a positive effect on you, leading you to see such persons with new eyes. It might be that this blessing is a sign of protection, guarding you against being wounded by the difficulties such people present in your life. For blessing others can bring you to think differently about them. It invites you to see them not simply as difficult persons who get on your nerves, but rather as those like you whom God has blessed. For they too are persons yearning to be who they truly are, and seeking to live at peace with themselves and others.

December 8
MARY IMMACULATE

TODAY IS THE FEAST of the Immaculate Conception, a celebration of Mary who as the Mother of God was conceived and born without sin. This teaching might seem strange to modern Christians, but the truth it conveys is that Mary is an example of one who has been redeemed, and from the very beginning of her life. When we celebrate Mary on this day, we are also celebrating our own lives, since this feast day reminds us that there is something pure and unstained in each of us from the start.

Mary is a woman who lived and loved without scheming or false intentions. In this sense, she is unlike us, who often fail in this regard: even when we do the good, it seems we often do so based on the wrong intentions. Too often our motivation for such acts reflects our desire to be esteemed by others, to put ourselves at the center of things. Too often we come face-to-face with the false intentions that inspire our attempts to love, insofar as we do so in order to be loved by others or recognized and honored by them.

The church's celebration of this feast reminds us that we are not only sinners born into this sin-infected world. For with Mary we also realize that the part of us where Christ dwells remains without sin and guilt. It is not stained with intrigue and false motives, but remains pure and without blemish. The reading from the Letter to the Ephesians expresses this poignantly:

> [God] chose us in Christ before the foundation of the world to be holy and blameless [or "immaculate," in the Latin version] before him in love. (Eph. 1:4)

There, in that place where Christ dwells within us, sin has no chance. There, we are without blemish. There, guilt can make no entrance into our lives. Even if we deserve to have guilt heaped on our shoulders, there remains an innermost part of our lives that remains unaffected by sin, a dimension that is holy and without blemish from the start.

In my work as a spiritual counselor I meet many people who share with me their experience of stumbling into some great sin in their lives. This has led them to denounce themselves as if they were terrible people, and their lives utterly ruined. For such persons, the Feast of the Immaculate Conception can bring a consoling message. It reminds us that our innermost heart has not been touched by sin. Despite the guilt we carry there remains within us, at our core, something pure and blameless. Our deepest identity remains unaffected by the guilt of our sin.

Our feelings of guilt cannot penetrate the heart of our identity. There, we cannot damage ourselves in the ways we judge and diminish ourselves.

🐝 Practice

Sit down quietly and spend some time thinking about the inner chaos of your feelings—your frustrations, your envy and jealousy, your fear and sadness, and the guilt you feel all the way to the center of your soul. Imagine that beneath the weight of all this inner chaos there remains, in your true heart, a quiet place that is clean and pure, which your feelings of guilt and self-judgment cannot penetrate. Christ dwells there, in the ground of your soul. And where Christ dwells, you are and remain pure and without blemish. Savor this purity within yourself. You know that in your thoughts, feelings, and deeds there is much that is unclean. But in the ground of your soul, in your heart, is a purity that enables you to sense your own worthiness.

December 9
FORGIVENESS

John the Baptist appeared in the wilderness, proclaiming a baptism of repentance for the forgiveness of sins. (Mk. 1:4)

MANY OF US CANNOT FORGIVE ourselves for having failed to fulfill the expectations we had for ourselves, or for some failure of ours that tarnished our self-image. We'd hoped to make a good impression on others perhaps, and now find that we're filled with self-blame for our failings. Perhaps we even imagine that everyone else has noticed we're not the good person we'd wanted to be.

Some of us have a hard time forgiving others who've hurt us. We close ourselves off, not wanting to have anything more to do with such persons. In the process, our hurt begins to weigh us down until we feel as if we're carrying it with us all the time and everywhere we go.

When we experience true forgiveness, however, we feel ourselves invited to offer it to others. For forgiveness means being freed first of all from the power of others. When I find I can't forgive others, I remain bound to them—as if stuck circling around them with my anger, hurt, or disappointment.

Forgiveness, then, is a twofold act of liberation. I must first be freed from the negative energy I experienced in being hurt, which is a kind of self-cleansing. Only then can I free myself from the power of the other, finding myself released from being bound to them. Forgiveness is about learning to let go of that which might just as well remain with the other.

At times, we find ourselves oppressed by our own hurtful behavior toward others. In such circumstances, Advent offers us a good opportunity to ask others for forgiveness and cleanse old conflicts so that we might come to celebrate a peaceful Christmas together.

ᘒᕁ Practice

Jesus forgave his murderers from the cross and prayed for them:

Father, forgive them; for they do not know what they are doing. (Lk. 23:34)

Take time this morning to pray these words for ten full minutes, first of all for yourself, thinking especially about the ways you aren't able to forgive yourself: "Father, forgive me, for I didn't know what I was doing, and don't know what I'm doing." After praying this simple claim for a time, you'll begin to feel a sense of peace growing within you. Your self-accusations might well dwindle away and disappear altogether.

Next, think of those who've hurt you recently, or those with whom you have a hard time getting along. As you call such persons to mind, pray this for them: "*Father, forgive them, for they didn't know what they were doing.*" It may well be that you'll initially experience a resistance to saying this with all your full heart, and find yourself thinking: "*But they knew exactly what they were doing! They tried to hurt me intentionally.*" Continue to pray for them, and see if you begin to sense that even if they'd tried to hurt you, they didn't truly understand what they were doing—and didn't see how they were simply inflicting their own hurt on you. After ten or fifteen minutes, you'll begin to sense how praying in this manner can begin to change you and your relationship to them.

December 10
PREPARE THE WAY

JOHN THE BAPTIST voiced this admonition to those who came to him:

Prepare the way of the Lord. (Mk. 1:3)

He was quoting the ancient prophet Isaiah, whose words summoned the people of Israel in their captivity in Babylon. There, in that distant land, they felt homesick for their lost Jerusalem. Great mountains now separated them from their beloved city, with no broad streets crossing the distances but only difficult and winding paths. The prophet's words were intended to stir up courage among the vanquished Israelites. They were the ones called to "prepare a way for the Lord," and make straight his paths.

It seems that Isaiah took this image directly from what he experienced during this captivity in Babylon, where broad and majestic streets served as the place of ceremonial processions for their gods. Such a street is what the Israelites should prepare for their Lord so that he might come to them and lead them home again. This was to fulfill the prophecy Isaiah had written elsewhere:

So the ransomed of the Lord shall return
and come to Zion with singing;
everlasting joy shall be upon their heads;
they shall obtain joy and gladness,
and sorrow and sighing shall flee away. (Isa. 51:11)

❧ Practice

How could you "prepare the way" of the Lord in your life so that God might come into your heart, to liberate and save you? What decisions or tasks have you put off doing? Perhaps such things have become like stones in your path that cause you to trip and fall. Imagine, then, God coming to you in the midst of these burdens with his love and beauty. Is the way to your heart open for his coming? Or have you walled yourself in to keep him at a distance? If so, break down those walls, setting aside the obstacles in your life to make room for God to come in. And when God does come, then shall the prophecy of Isaiah be fulfilled: "They shall obtain joy and gladness, and sorrow and sighing shall flee away."

December 11
MOVING MOUNTAINS

JOHN THE BAPTIST came preaching these words:

Every valley shall be filled,
and every mountain and hill shall be made low,
and the crooked shall be made straight,
and the rough ways made smooth. (Lk. 3:5)

We often speak about having a "mountain of work" before us. In the face of such a burden, we often don't know where to begin, having the feeling that we can never accomplish what needs to be done. The "mountain" we face seems to overwhelm us, as if it might crush and bury us at any moment. In such times, the prophetic words that "every mountain and hill shall be made low" might come as truly good news. The image is a strong one, suggesting that immeasurable tons of earth will fall down before God so that a "straight" road might be built and the rough places made plain.

We know in our lives that things can go wrong and become "crooked." Perhaps we're bent over from the weight of the burdens we carry. Perhaps we didn't always act in ways that were forthright and proper, or let ourselves be "bent" to accept things we knew were wrong—which is often easier than standing up to oppose such obstacles in our lives. But when this happens, things don't actually get easier for us. On the contrary, we might well begin to feel uncomfortable in our own skin. In such times, the Advent promise that "the crooked shall be made straight" can encourage us. In such times, we hear the words of the prophet as encouragement when he describes how "every mountain and hill" will be brought low so that God might enter our lives on a straight and smooth path.

❧ Practice

Today, take time to imagine concretely what it would mean to bring down a "mountain" in your life. Think about the things you've been putting off doing, decisions you should have made but haven't yet attended to. What would it take to tackle such tasks and face the things you've been avoiding? How might you begin to do this today? Perhaps it's something as small as cleaning your room, or making a call you needed to make but had avoided for some time. Once you begin attending to such things, you'll see how much better off you'll be. You'll have begun to move mountains. You'll soon be able to go about your day without the stress of such worries, finding yourself greatly relieved.

The mountain you've just moved might also ease things in your relationship with God. Rather than constantly asking *God* to remove such burdens in your life, you've now begun to take this on yourself. In this way you'll begin to find yourself becoming open for the God who desires to come into your life and speak with you. This is the Lord who yearns to reveal himself to you in the stillness of Advent, beyond all the hurry and worry, so that your heart might be filled with true peace.

December 12
CLEANSING

JOHN THE BAPTIST called those who'd come to listen to him to be baptized for the forgiveness of their sins. The practice of being immersed in the waters of the Jordan River as a cleansing of sin answered their longing for purity of life. These people felt that they'd turned from God in their lives, and came to experience their sin as something unclean that needed to be removed. Their sins had made them unclean, leaving them stained and soiled.

A Protestant minister recently told me that every time he'd been interrogated by the secret police in the former East Germany, he'd afterward felt the need to shower and cleanse himself. He wanted to wash away the filth he felt clinging to him from the dirty tactics these officials used. All of us know something of this yearning to cleanse ourselves from what has stained our hearts. We long for what monks in ancient times called "purity of heart." We yearn for a clean heart that enables us to love without false intentions or ulterior motives.

The monks of old practiced purity of heart by refusing to judge others or pass blame on them. To do this they had to struggle with their emotions and thoughts, with their passions and desires, in order that such things would no longer control them and they might come to experience inner freedom. Purity of heart was the condition that enabled them to love without false intentions.

❧ Practice

When you take your next shower, imagine that the warm water not only cleanses your body but also washes away all that stains your soul. Imagine this water flowing over you as a sign of God's love, which is able to cleanse you of all that's unclean in your life: unkind thoughts you've had toward others; speaking badly of others, which hurts both them and yourself; ambivalent excuses you've made; questionable things you've done.

Next, imagine that God's love is not simply like the water that streams over your body. Rather, it penetrates your soul to cleanse all the dust and dirt that has accumulated in your inner life.

How might you take concrete measures to act on this? Today, try to avoid speaking badly of others and, above all, passing judgment on them.

December 13
TWO BEARERS OF LIGHT:
ST. ODILIA AND ST. LUCY

TODAY THE CHURCH celebrates two female saints who've come to play a large role in the traditions of Advent: St. Odilia and St. Lucy.

Both of these women are associated with light. According to ancient traditions, St. Odilia was a woman who'd gone blind but upon being baptized received her sight again. Baptism healed her of her blindness.

This story reminds us that early Christians understood baptism not simply as a cleansing but also as an illumination. When we're baptized, we're "immersed" in Christ, and when we come to have a deep experience of Christ in our lives, we begin to see the world around us with new eyes. Our inner eyes are "illumined." One might say that we, too, are healed of a kind of blindness, and thus enabled to see the world as God does. Faith gives us back this vision we often lose along the way.

What of St. Lucy—or *Santa Lucia*—who's often referred to as a "light bearer"? We find her represented in art and folk traditions as carrying a lamp or candle in her hand. In Sweden, in fact, she is celebrated with a great festival and public processions in which a young woman representing her comes dressed in a white dress and wearing a crown of lights.

The tradition has it that Lucy, as a young woman, wanted to live the consecrated life of a virgin so that she could devote herself entirely to the light of Christ. As the story goes, she was actually brought to trial for her refusal to give up this desire, and sentenced by a judge to work in a bordello. But after he rendered his verdict no one could move her from where she stood. She was then doused with scalding oil, but even this didn't harm her. The soldiers then threw her into the midst of a raging fire, but as the flames arched over her she was miraculously protected by a wall that formed around her and above her head.

The story tells of St. Lucy's steadfast and complete trust in God, and her role as a person who reflected God's face to others. The fire of passions and desires couldn't harm her, for she lived through the power of a stronger love: that is, the love of God.

Both women present themselves to us as symbols of Advent, reminding us of God's light, which heals us of our inner blindness and illumines us in the darkness of our hearts.

Just as the burning candles of the Advent wreathe brighten the darkness of the world, so, too, St. Odilia and St. Lucy are witnesses to the hope that Christ's coming might be a light for our path, one

shining in a dark place, until the day dawns and the morning star rises in [our] hearts. (2 Pet. 1:19)

The light of Advent seeks first to illumine our eyes. It wants to penetrate our very bodies so that we might become light ourselves, without blind spots or the darkness of sin. The story of Lucy reminds us that we should be witnesses to this light by igniting the light of our love against the darkness we find in our world, letting it burn in unexpected places. This might be where others have given themselves over to their desires and passions, where they want to burn others with their hate, or in those places where nothing of God is visible. We pray that the little light of our faith might burn even in places like these, so that love might bring a bit of light and warmth into our often dark and cold world.

✾ Practice

Find a place to sit quietly. Light a candle in front of you, and imagine as its light penetrates your body and soul that you yourself are to become light in the darkness. For as Jesus reminds us:

> *Your eye is the lamp of your body. If your eye is healthy, your whole body is full of light. (Lk. 11:34)*

Imagine, for a moment, that your eyes are so pure that light actually streams forth from them. With this in mind, approach others today without making judgments about them or wasting their time. Let them be as they are.

Look for beauty in each one of them. When you do, it will seem that light is radiating from your eyes. Imagine being for each person you'll meet a source of God's light, illumining their lives so that there might be a brightness all around and within them.

III

THE THIRD SUNDAY
OF ADVENT

Rejoice!

The Gospel reading for the third Sunday of Advent centers again on John the Baptist. Matthew tells us of how John sent emissaries to Jesus, asking,

> *Are you the one who is to come, or are we to wait for another?*
> *(Matt. 11:3)*

In answer to this query, Jesus points to the things he'd already accomplished: restoring sight to the blind and letting the lame walk, cleansing the lepers and restoring to the deaf their hearing. Then Jesus went on to praise John as the greatest among all people. But that said, he adds that even the humblest in the kingdom of heaven was greater than John. This suggests to us how, through our encounter with Christ, we find ourselves in another dimension altogether, one that transcends John's preaching of conversion. For Luke tells that John preached to tax collectors, soldiers, and simple people in order to tell them what they should do. But John the Evangelist, in his Gospel, goes further than this, portraying John the Baptist as the prophet who points to Jesus as the Messiah who is to come after him:

> *Among you stands one whom you do not know, the one who is coming after me; I am not worthy to untie the thong of his sandal. (John 1:26–27)*

This third Sunday in Advent is shaped not by John's preaching of conversion but by the call to joy: the opening words of worship on this day begin with the word *Gaudete*, or "Rejoice!" This is why we call this the "*Gaudete* Sunday," the Sunday of rejoicing. On this day, priests and ministers wear pink vestments, a foreshadowing of the Christmas joy that will be proclaimed for all people. The Introit recalls Paul's words in his Letter to the Philippians, where the apostle writes from prison to admonish his brothers:

> *Rejoice in the Lord always; again I will say, Rejoice. Let your gentleness be known to everyone. The Lord is near. (Phil. 4:4–5)*

Of course, we know that many among us—and often enough we ourselves—find the call to rejoice a difficult one to hear. After all, one cannot be *commanded* to rejoice. It seems something we should not have to do as a duty. But this is not what the apostle meant. His intent was to warn his fellow Christians not to become immobilized by their fear of death, which clearly threatened him in prison. Nor were they to worry about the difficulties they would face in this world. Rather, they should take heart, knowing that the Lord was near. And insofar as they could experience the Lord's nearness, the apostle knew that joy would be born within them. The wisdom of his experience speaks in his admonition to rejoice.

Paul had tasted the nearness of God in his life as a source of great joy. And it's true: when we sense that the Lord is near, the possibility of being hurt by those around us no longer seems quite as threatening. Nor do the conflicts that might otherwise seem capable of overwhelming us. To be near Jesus was the apostle's deepest longing. Of course, Paul knew that *Jesus* was always near. But it often seems to us, when we're honest about it, that *we* are far from him. And when we experience this distance, we find ourselves estranged from our true self and removed from others. And as long as we're not at home with ourselves, not present to our true selves, we fail to experience this nearness of Jesus.

The recognition that the Lord is near invites us to come home to ourselves, in order to welcome him into our hearts. This is what it takes for joy to grow in us and bring us a sense of being fully alive and truly free. Grasped by such a joy, we find we're able to be with others with greater understanding and kindness. When we feel that Jesus is near we begin to see the goodness of others more clearly, and thus begin to learn how to get along with them better.

The nearness of the Lord frees us of our worries, which is no small thing, because as an old saying puts it, "the human person is a worry." Here, the German word for worry, *Sorge*, has two meanings. On the one hand, it means "grief, sorrow, fear, tormenting thoughts." But on the other it can also mean "to seek help." Many of us torment ourselves with worry. We worry about whether we'll be financially secure in the future. We worry about our retirement. We worry about our problems, or those we might have to face in the future, and so on. Even in Advent we find ourselves beset with worry: we worry about not finding the right presents, or not being able to celebrate Christmas joyfully because some nagging conflict might well disrupt the peace of this season.

Jesus called his disciples to a life uncluttered with worrying, for he knew that God would provide for them—and for us—since he provides for the birds of the heavens and gives the lilies of the field what they need (see Matt. 6:25–34). Advent is a season that promises to free us from our anxieties and let us practice what it means to trust God in everything. Rather than giving in to the worries that threaten us, we're to let go of our troubles and, with prayers and petitions but also with thanks to God, be assured that he cares for us.

The nearness of the Lord we hear praised in the hymns we sing on this third Advent Sunday seek to lead us into joy, beyond a life fraught with anxiety. For when we find that the Lord is near to us, we experience the fulfillment of our deepest longings. This is the message we hear, too, in our worship on this day. The question is whether this remains a truth we only know to speak in pious words, or whether we're able to sense in our hearts that the Lord is truly near—to *us*, as Teresa of Avila put it in the words of the familiar Taizé setting:

> *Let nothing disturb you, let nothing frighten you. . . . Whoever has God lacks nothing; God alone suffices. (Teresa of Avila, "Nada te turbe")*

When I give myself in the stillness of my heart to the Lord's nearness, I find strength in the conviction that this word is really true for *me*. For I lack nothing when I sense God's presence within me. When this happens, I feel my heart being widened, and my fears and worries falling away. I come to know that this is what I long for, that when the Lord himself is near, when the one who loves me is in my heart, I am completely filled with his unending love.

When I come to have this experience, joy fills my heart. I no longer have to be admonished to rejoice, for joy is simply real in my life. But I also know that the day's pressures might well darken this experience, and then I'll need to hear the apostle's word as a *command* and heed his call to rejoice—because, in spite of everything, the Lord is near even when I don't sense it.

December 14
GOOD DEEDS

WHEN THE PEOPLE went out in the wilderness to John the Baptist, they came to him asking:

What then should we do? (Lk. 3:10)

This question is typical in the writings of ancient Greek philosophers. But their first question was the more fundamental one: *Who are we?* The Christmas message is an answer to this primary question, telling us that we're people of divine worth precisely because in Jesus's coming God became human among us. Their second question, then, was the same one raised by those who came to John the Baptist: *What should we do?* John's answer makes clear that those who came to him could not avoid facing their need for conversion, an experience that prepares the way for the Lord's coming.

The first command John the Baptist announced to those who came to hear him was this: *Take what you have and share it with others.*" The tax collectors of his day, who had a reputation as sinners because of how they conducted their work, also came to hear John. But notice this: he didn't tell them to quit their work, but rather told them to cease extorting from people more than they owed. He told soldiers that they shouldn't mishandle persons, and be satisfied with their wages. Such concrete examples point to how we, too, are to prepare ourselves for Jesus's coming, how we are to open ourselves to him in our lives. Advent is a season of our own preparation, inviting us to consider our actions and ask how—in concrete terms—we might prepare a way for Jesus's coming through conversion of life and renouncing the often unconscious failings in our lives.

❧ Practice

Begin your day by asking yourself this: "*What can I do today to 'prepare the way of the Lord'? What good deed, large or small, might I undertake to this end?*" When I was growing up, my siblings and I used to begin each day in Advent by asking ourselves what good deed we might do that day. Perhaps this meant cleaning up the dishes after a meal or helping our little sister with her homework. For every good deed we did we were allowed to place one piece of hay in the manger of our nativity set. Of course, we wanted to make sure that by the time Christmas came, the Christ child would not have to be placed in a rough and empty manger, but rather in one filled with the hay we'd brought because of the good deeds we'd done during the weeks of Advent.

Take a few moments to think about your own life. Surely you can imagine some act of kindness you could do today that exceeds what might normally be expected of you. Perhaps this would be to visit someone you know, to reach out to bring some small joy to a person in need, to call or send a note to a friend or acquaintance. In ways like these you can imagine, in concrete ways, how you might live the message of Advent in your life.

December 15
JOY

Rejoice in the Lord always. (Phil. 4:4)

PAUL WROTE THESE WORDS about rejoicing from his prison cell. In his day, it was never clear that prisoners would ever come out alive. But the apostle paid no attention to this danger, trusting that the Lord was near to him—and knowing that this alone was sufficient cause for joy. That confidence is what inspired him, in his letter to the Christians of Philippi, to tell them they should rejoice in God.

It's important to say that this joy isn't simply a matter of some feeling. It should express itself in the kindness we show toward those we know. For joy is an elevated emotion, as psychologists remind us, which has a positive effect on our lives. And while it is true that we can't rejoice on demand, we know that within each of us lies a source of joy waiting to be found.

We rejoice when we succeed at accomplishing something great in our lives. We can also rejoice each day over some small encounter we experience. When we hear these prophetic words during Advent, we find ourselves stirred by the source of joy, and our sense of Jesus's nearness is just such a source, even though it's often hidden under layers of worry and concern because of our troubles. And when we give in to the hurry that too often presses us, we find ourselves utterly unable to receive this joy, even when it is daily offered.

We need a sense of mindfulness in order to learn to rejoice in the small things of life. This takes time and inner intentionality so that we might discover the deepest source of joy in our hearts.

🐝 Practice

Find a quiet place where you can sit, and listen to what's stirring in your heart. What feelings do you sense arising within you? Welcome them, even if they might at first seem unpleasant to you.

Ask yourself whether there might be some joy hidden beneath the weight of such feelings. And consider this: What has already brought joy your way this day? What joy might come to you in the particular things that await you today? Can you find a source of joy in your health? In your family? In the many encounters you'll experience this day? Or will all this simply pass you by? Remember these words of Jesus, and say them softly in your heart:

I have said these things to you so that my joy may be in you, and that your joy may be complete. (John 15:11)

Imagine making room for these words in your life; let them be a source of joy for you. Imagine them flowing into the center of your heart and rising up slowly until you find your mind filled with them. Be patient with this practice. When you experience some measure of it, you'll no longer find it difficult or overwhelming to rejoice. Joy will simply well up within you, so that you cannot help but experience it.

Go into this day open for this experience, ready to rejoice over the smallest things—an encounter with someone you'll meet; a smile from a stranger on the bus; the friendliness of a salesperson in a store; the time you'll take for yourself after your day is finished and you enter a church to sit quietly and savor the stillness you find there.

December 16
THE LORD IS NEAR

THE GROUND OF JOY, as the apostle Paul reminds us, is the Lord's nearness to us. He experienced this while he was in the hostile setting of a prison. But he was so convinced that the Lord was with him that the guards' threatening behavior didn't disturb him. He knew he was safe because the Lord was near.

This sense of God's presence was for Paul reason enough for joy. He rejoiced that, even though locked up in a prison sell, he was not alone. Jesus was with him. He experienced Jesus's nearness in everything, even in his suffering, because through it Paul came to share something with him. For by sharing in Christ's suffering he experienced a sense of communion with the Lord.

The sense of God's nearness was a profound experience for the apostle Paul, enabling him to sense how Jesus's love surrounded him like a warm, protective cloak against the cold of his prison cell. This took away his fear and filled him with boundless joy. This was the gift he wished to share with his fellow Christians in Philippi.

ᴥ Practice

The nearness of God is like a protective cloak that guards us from being needled by those around us, who might wish us ill. Today, when you put your coat on to go outside, say to yourself: *"When I put my coat on, I am putting Christ on as my cloak, and this cloak is good for me. Through it I feel myself loved and safely held. It will guard me today against hurtful words or the restlessness and hurry I'll encounter in the city."*

When you return from work, wrap yourself in a warm blanket and imagine that just as this blanket gives you a feeling of well-being, so too does Jesus's love surround you and give you a sense of being safe, accepted, loved, and protected. As you wrap yourself in this blanket, say quietly: *"Now I need nothing more. I can just be. The sense of pure being I feel fills me with joy. I feel free. I don't have to fulfill anyone else's expectations. I'm under no pressure to do anything. I can simply savor and enjoy the warming love of Jesus."*

December 17
SEEKING A PLACE OF REFUGE

LUKE TELLS US that Mary laid the child in a manger,

because there was no place for them in the inn. (Lk. 2:7)

Over the centuries, popular devotion created a vivid scene depicting Joseph and Mary in their search for room in an inn. In many Christmas pageants, we watch as they go knocking door to door, only to be turned away again and again. In the beautiful region of Tyrol, in Austria, one often hears a lovely folksong that still has the power to stir our heart:

Who is knocking? —Oh, two poor people on their way.
What do they want?—Oh, give us a room in an inn today.

The search for such a room seems timely given the vast stream of refugees coming to Europe in recent years. Their presence among us does not mean that everyone should be required to take them into their homes, but the season of Advent reminds us of those in our midst who are seeking refuge from the violence of their war-torn homelands. Of course, there are others seeking "shelter" of another sort, whose plight is not that of fleeing from a strange land, but rather a flight from themselves. They might well fear the solitude of this season, afraid that it could expose the truth about their unlived life. They might feel themselves required to face the reality of their life with honesty.

All who are in flight from their true self, who are trying to escape silence or avoid the truth about their lives, need a place of refuge. They need to feel safe and secure, to find a "room" where they can sense some measure of peace in the midst of their fear.

❧ Practice

Take time today to take a long look at your life, asking yourself this: *"Am I in a place of refuge where I feel safe and secure? Do I feel held and supported lovingly by God? Am I 'at home' in my family, feeling truly comfortable there? Can I treasure my 'room' (or home) as a place where I feel at peace with the world? Am I truly alive in my room (or home), or do I just exist there?"*

Look around the place where you live. How would you like to decorate it today so that you might feel more at home here?

Then consider people around you who might be seeking refuge and feeling utterly alone in these days before Christmas. What opportunities might you envision to offer them a sense of refuge? This need not require you to open your home to them. But it could be that you know someone who feels alone or abandoned in this season. You might send them a card or a small gift, or invite them to join you in celebrating Christmas in your church.

December 18
ANGELS

ANGELS PLAY A LARGE role in Advent and Christmas. In Luke's telling of the story, an angel announces to Zechariah that he is to be the father of a son. An angel comes to Mary with the promise that she will conceive a child by the Holy Spirit who will be called the son of God. An angel of the Lord approaches the shepherds in their fields, telling them of the great joy they are to experience, namely, that a savior will be born in the city of David. And a heavenly host of angels pushes this messenger aside in order to give voice to the Christmas message of praise:

Glory to God in the highest heaven,
and on earth peace among those whom he favors. (Lk. 2:14)

An angel also appears to Joseph in a dream, telling him what had happened to Mary, his betrothed: that the son she is carrying was conceived of the Holy Spirit. He goes on to tell Joseph exactly what he is to do: he should take Mary as his wife, and after the birth flee with them to Egypt in order to avoid Herod's deadly plot. Once in Egypt, an angel appears to Joseph again, this time telling him to return home. Joseph listened to the angel and did as he was told.

The Christmas season is a time when the boundary between heaven and earth seems to fall away, and angels are often responsible for this. They bring God into close contact with the people. It's not without cause, then, that we decorate our homes with angels in this season, for they're the ones who show us that God is near. That the Lord accompanies us in the concrete activities of our daily lives. That he brings us guidance in dreams and, in protecting us, breaks wide our inner barriers so that we might open our hearts for God.

Angels are all around us. As the tradition suggests, they are without weight, having spiritual bodies, thereby modeling for us what it means to take our lives more lightly. Angels play in order to help us become more playful in our lives. They share with us the tender breath of God's love. We're surrounded by angels who let the praises of God ring in our hearts, encouraging us to sense that the God who is "in the highest heaven" is also close to us here on earth, and longs to share with us his peace.

❧ Practice

Consider where and when and how you might already have encountered your guardian angel. Where did you find yourself guarded from an accident, or protected from some great harm? Who has been for you an angel, a messenger who brought you the right word at the moment you needed to hear it? A word that kept you going through hard times?

Angels can come to us in our conversation with others. Angels can be the impulses we feel within us, the urges we hear with an inner ear but often ignore or try to silence. Take a moment to listen for these inner messages today. It may well be that an angel is trying to speak with you, even now.

Perhaps an angel is also encouraging you to become such a messenger for someone you know. For when you truly attend to this voice speaking in your heart, you might find yourself becoming an "angel" for another. Of course, it is not for you to let on that this is happening. But you can be grateful that you have been chosen, in spite of your weaknesses and failures, to be an angel for someone in your life.

December 19
THE STUMP

A TEXT WE HEAR read during Advent speaks of a tree that has been cut down:

> *A shoot shall come out from the stump of Jesse,*
> *and a branch shall grow out of his roots.*
> *The spirit of the Lord shall rest on him,*
> *the spirit of wisdom and understanding,*
> *the spirit of counsel and might,*
> *the spirit of knowledge and the fear of the Lord. (Isa. 11.1–2)*

Artists have delighted in making paintings of the so-called stump of Jesse, for according to the Scriptures many kings and prophets came forth from this root along with one final "branch," Jesus Christ. He is the sprout that springs forth from the sawed-off stump, an image we hear celebrated in a popular German Christmas carol:

> *Lo, how a rose e'er blooming*
> *From tender stem hath sprung!*
> *Of Jesse's lineage coming*
> *as men of old have sung.*

This image of a stump sawed off at the root that in time brings forth new branches and blossoms is a vivid symbol of hope for us. For we've all experienced gaps in our lives when things were cut away—relationships that fell apart; the failure of the ambitions we had for our lives; the loss of a job.

The message of this prophetic text is this: no failure of ours is without the possibility of a new beginning. There is no breach that cannot lead to an experience of new life. And when something is cut off in our lives, something new can come forth—when the roots are healthy. Advent is the season when we find ourselves called upon to sink our roots deep in faith, roots that not only are ours but also belong to our family lineage. These are the roots we live from, inherited from our parents and grandparents and those who went before them.

⚹ Practice

Take time today to walk in the woods, or in a park, and take a moment to examine the roots you'll find there. These might even be in your own yard. Take a close look at them and ask yourself: *"What are my own roots? How are my parents, grandparents, and great-grandparents roots in my life? Am I even aware of my roots, or am I cut off from them somehow? Are my roots hurting with injuries?"*

Consider how it is that when the roots are healthy, the plant can give forth new shoots that will yield fruit in their season. Think about how you might bring the roots of your life to the Christmas manger in your nativity set. In Germany, it is a common tradition for people to gather moss in the forests or near their house and use it to cover the ground around the manger of their nativity set, and to decorate it with small evergreen branches. This reminds us of how our roots carry life within us and are able to bring forth fruit in our lives. For even if something has been cut off from these roots, they can yet break open with new life again. Through the power of these roots in your life, a blessing can go forth from you for those who are around you.

December 20
SWORDS TO PLOWSHARES

DURING ADVENT, we hear marvelous words from the prophets, among them this saying from the prophet Isaiah:

They shall beat their swords into plowshares,
and their spears into pruning hooks. (Isa. 2:4)

Many who read these words might well think that they're too beautiful to be true, that such a claim is sheer fantasy. But there is creative power in this text, and if we trust it, it has the power to change us and our society.

A pastor I know, Christian Führer, currently leads the worship services on Mondays in the famous St. Nicholas Church in Leipzig, but as a minister in the former East Germany he'd been an active leader in the peace movement there. He once shared this story with me. Every book published in that country during Communist times had to be authorized by the government, but no law existed with regard to printing things on fabric. The East German peace movement took advantage of this loophole and printed these three words on cloth patches: "Swords to plowshares." Young people sewed them on their jeans and jackets, and even on their sweaters. And these three simple words on such patches were so threatening to this government with all their tanks and shows of military might that police were charged with the task of removing them by force. Of course, this made them look absurd—that the mighty state would be so afraid of three little words. But what power they had!

This example points to the explosive power of the prophetic words we read or hear during this season. We must simply learn to trust them. For God is still speaking such words of promise to us today, and insofar as we take them to heart, their power comes to work in us, able to change us and the atmosphere in which we live.

When I hear these words during Advent, I open my heart to them and let them speak to me, saying: "*This is what is truly real. There is something beyond the news I hear or read every day. This world stands under the promises of God, and God can still work wonders today.*"

❧ Practice

Consider the ways in which you might make swords into plowshares in your life. Think of the people you know at your job, in school, or in your neighborhood whom you have a hard time getting along with. Perhaps they're people you avoid.

Make some symbol or paint a simple picture that depicts what it might look like to take a sword and make a plowshare out of it. Draw a dove of peace. Or buy a card with some image or symbol that conveys a sense of peace and reconciliation, either in words or by means of a picture. Give this card (or image or symbol) to one of these persons. You might see how an unexpected gift can soften the tensions between you, even to the point that you suddenly sense a new way of being with them.

IV

THE FOURTH SUNDAY
OF ADVENT

Let it Be with Me According to Your Word!

The fourth Advent Sunday places Mary once again in the center of the story. The Evangelist Mathew tells us how, from Joseph's vantage point, we might consider Jesus's birth, since he himself was confused about this startling news. A dream came to him, helping him come to terms with it: it revealed to him that Mary, his betrothed, was to bear a child who would free the people of their sin. This child, he came to discover, was to be called Emmanuel, a name that means "God with us."

Christ desires to be born in each of us as well. But for this new birth to happen in our hearts, we need what Mary and Joseph had. We need the motherly womb of Mary in which God's Word took flesh, for, like Mary, we must also learn to take God's word into our lives, in faith, so that this Word might take form within us.

But we also need Joseph, who listened to his dreams. For in our dreams God often shows us what he hopes to do in our lives. He wants to show us that he is not merely a God who is far off, but one who lives within us, filling our hearts with his light and love.

Joseph also stands for the protection we must foster for the receptivity of the feminine side, represented by Mary, a dimension each of us carries within our hearts. We need a measure of Joseph's manly strength to find the discipline we need to do what God asks of us, so that God can grow within us and shape our lives completely.

Luke tells the story of the angel's annunciation to Mary. But God sends us angels as well, to tell us what he intends for us. Such an angel could come to us in the form of another person offering us guidance in our lives. But an angel might also come to us in a dream, showing us the next steps we should take.

As modern people we often doubt the notion of angels, or overlook those whom God sends our way. But Mary opened herself to the angel who came to her, and though she initially feared what this messenger shared with her, she went on to ponder in her heart what it all could have meant. She thought about how the angel's promise could become a concrete reality in her life. She didn't simply want to believe, but rather wanted to understand what she believed.

When the angel told her that the Holy Spirit would come over her, and that for God nothing was impossible, she answered: *"Here am I, the servant of the Lord; let it be with me according to your word"* (Lk. 1:38).

This is a confident response. Here, Mary doesn't diminish herself in speaking of herself as a "servant"; she is not one who simply says "Yes!" and "Let it be so!" to every request made of her. Rather, she's a woman who represents Israel, speaking her "Yes!" to God on behalf of Israel. Through it all, she trusts in God's promises despite how strange they might have seemed to her. For in the face of Israel's disobedience, Mary opened her life to God and came to embody an obedient Israel.

From her we learn to say "Yes!" to what God entrusts with us. We shouldn't belittle ourselves here, for God intends to do great things in our lives; he desires to be born within us as well. For when we trust God's will for our lives, the unique and special image God has of us will become stronger and clearer. But this requires that we learn to open ourselves, with all our strength, to receive God's Word, to take it into our lives so that his Word might also become flesh in our lives.

Luke tells another wonderful story about Mary when he describes her encounter with Elizabeth. He tells of how Mary set out to cross the mountains, refusing to stay at home. She carried Christ with her to the people, going to meet her cousin Elizabeth, who was also pregnant.

This is a marvelous story, one that reveals the mystery of this encounter to us: when we open ourselves to others in our lives by overcoming our prejudices or projections, when we truly come to meet them where they live, only then is a true encounter possible that is capable of changing us both. For Elizabeth, this experience came when the child "leaped for joy" in her womb, as Luke describes it. In that moment, the child came to life within her, and she came to know her "inner child," realizing her own unique and original identity. She was "filled with the Holy Spirit," as the Gospel puts it.

In an encounter just like this, where we desire nothing from the other but simply want to be open for them and receive the secret they hold, we also come to experience the Holy Spirit. Through the Spirit Elizabeth recognized who Mary was, that she was the mother of her Lord. But this is true for every human encounter: we, too, might encounter the Lord in every person we meet, for each of them is the mother of Christ. This is not only true for those we've known for a long time. It's not only true of friends we know well. No, every face shines for us with the face of God.

But a true encounter is only possible when we reflect on the mystery of the other, when we with Elizabeth find ourselves filled with wonder that the mother of our Lord also comes to us.

Elizabeth blesses Mary and speaks well of her: "*Blessed are you among women*" (Lk. 1:42), which we could understand to mean: "You are touched by God, loved by God. Your fruitfulness and aliveness are gifts of God."

And Elizabeth calls Mary blessed: "*Blessed is she who believed that there would be a fulfillment of what was spoken to her by the Lord*" (Lk. 1:45). Mary is the true image of faith, of one who has been redeemed. This saying is true for us as well: we too are blessed and, like Mary, are able to bless others. For when we trust the word of God as Mary did, which also promises us great things, we come to experience faith as a source of great gladness.

The fourth Sunday in Advent points ahead to Christmas. We'll meet many people, and experience this celebration with our families. But it's not necessarily the case that our family and friends will encounter each other without prejudices getting in the way. It may not happen that we'll be open enough to see Christ in each other and so bless and cherish one another.

Why is this so difficult? One reason for this is that we're often driven by our need to measure ourselves against others. We try to figure out who's more successful, or who is better off. And we often devalue others in order to inflate our own ego.

In fact, at no other time of the year are there as many family fights as there are at Christmas. Sometimes, things go so far that we're not capable of experiencing each other for who we truly are. We can't begin to enter into this celebration, which after all is all about true encounter, about discovering the mystery present within the other.

At Christmas we are invited to ponder the mystery we see in the manger when we gaze upon the divine child lying there before us. But in that very moment, we should also remember to look at the people around us. Like Elizabeth, we should learn to see members of our family with the eyes of faith, with eyes opened by the Holy Spirit.

Only then are we able to see in all those gathered around us—not simply our relatives or friends and acquaintances, but in each and every one—the presence of Mary, who is to bear Christ. Only then can we see in them the mother of our Lord coming to visit us so that the child within might also "leap with joy." Only then might we come in touch again with the inner child we carry within us, with our true self, with Christ, who desires to be born in us.

December 21
MARY, THE EXAMPLE OF FAITH

MARY EXEMPLIFIES for us what it means to be a person of faith. She entrusts herself to God, and trusts God's word brought by the angel.

In this season, what matters most is that we learn from Mary to believe anew. For believing means simply this: to give ourselves fully to God's word. This holds true for the words we read in the Scriptures, for here God wants to address us in our lives today, to stir our hearts. But we must open our heart to this encounter, so that the Word might come into us, to change us.

God addresses us in the quietest impulses of the heart that come during prayer or worship, and in those hushed moments when we're able to truly listen within. But we often drown out these moments with arguments that weigh us down with the burden of useless thoughts: "*Well, that was surely conceited of me. That little thought that came to me just now can surely have nothing whatsoever to do with God.*"

In this case, we should not think of the angel's message in the ways artists have so often portrayed it, for if such a remarkable angel were to come suddenly into our midst, we would surely trust his message. But angels often speak in almost inaudible ways. We could learn from Mary how to obey such inner impulses as this, for she knew how to open herself in trust to the angel's words. And this utterly changed her life: she believed the impossible news she received from him, trusting his word that "*nothing will be impossible with God*" (Lk. 1:37). Or, as the original Greek puts it, "For every word, with God, is full of power; it accomplishes what it says."

Mary answers this messenger with courageous words: "*Here am I, the servant of the Lord; let it be with me according to your word*" (Lk. 1:38).

She had no idea, of course, what the consequences of this word would be for her. But she trusted that God intended only what was good for her.

❧ Practice

Take time to reflect on your faith in God. Perhaps you believe the message of the Scriptures in a general sense. But do you also trust that God can speak with you personally?

Say this question aloud, addressing it to God: "*Good Lord, what do you want me to do? What do you want of me? What do you entrust with me?*" And then listen in the stillness to see if an answer arises within you. You won't hear words spoken aloud, but thoughts might well rise up in your heart.

Consider these thoughts with great care and ask yourself whether God might not be speaking with you in this way. You must, of course, test these thoughts to discern whether they are of the Holy Spirit or whether they arise from your own pride, from your superego. How can you distinguish this? You'll know they're from God if they bring aliveness, freedom, peace, and love into your life.

Trust such thoughts, and say with Mary: "*See, I am ready to trust myself to you and to serve you. Let it be with me according to your word.*"

December 22
GOD'S BIRTH IN OUR SOUL

WHAT THE ANGEL announced to Mary might seem unbelievable to us when we read that the Holy Spirit "overshadowed" her: "*Therefore the child to be born will be holy; he will be called Son of God*" (Lk. 1:35). But this message might well hold true for us too. For we celebrate Christmas not simply as a remembrance that God was once born of Mary as a baby. Rather, and as the Christian mystics have reminded us all along, we celebrate in this season God's birth in our own souls. One of these, a poet who lived in the seventeenth century known as Angelus Silesius, expressed this in a memorable way:

> *If Christ had been a thousand times in Bethlehem born,*
> *but not in you, then you're lost and for eternity forlorn.*

What does it mean to say that God can be born within us? This is a manner of speaking that points to a reality we can only imagine through language like this. What the poet means is that when God is born in us, we come to touch the unstained and unique image that God has of us. God has such an image for each of us, but it is an image that has often been weakened within us—because of the false images others have foisted on us, images coming from negative thoughts we have of ourselves, or inflated notions we have of our own importance. Of course, we have no means of expressing what this image looks like concretely, but we know that when we come in contact with it and discover again the deep inner peace alive in our hearts, we come to realize that we're in harmony with ourselves.

For when God is born within us, we discover our real self. We arrive at our own true center. When God who is mystery comes to dwell in us, we find we're able to come home to ourselves. For God, as the church fathers often remind us, is born within us in silence. This is why it's so important that we take time during Advent and at Christmas to devote ourselves to times of stillness so that we might discover this truth in ourselves. For only when we keep silent can we begin to sense that our innermost heart is a quiet place in which God might be born within us and renew our life completely.

❧ Practice

Find a place and time to sit quietly by yourself. Cross your arms on your chest as a symbolic way of protecting the place of inner stillness within you, imagining that no other person has access to that inner realm. Not even the many thoughts that are constantly running through your head nor the hurtful words of others or your own self-accusing thoughts can penetrate this quiet place in your heart. God himself dwells in this place, in the depths of your heart. But God is there like a little child who often remains unnoticed, for you can't ever fully grasp him. You can only touch him softly, in the stillness, like you might stroke a newborn baby. Now say to yourself: *"If God is within me, then I am utterly free of the need to compare myself with others. I am allowed to be truly who I am— which is to say, imperfect. I no longer need to justify myself or prove myself. I'm allowed to be who I am, and to know that I am a limited, mistake-prone person."* As Carl Jung put it, we too are present in the stall where God wants to be born. For there, in the manger in the center of our soul, lies the divine child. And that utterly changes things for me, giving me the feeling that I am at one with myself in the depths of my soul.

December 23
ENCOUNTER

MARY SET OUT on her journey to visit her cousin Elizabeth when she was already pregnant. Christmas is a celebration when we come to know what it means to encounter one another as Mary and Elizabeth did. Like Mary, we need to go forth on our own way, crossing the mountains we face in our lives, getting beyond the peaks of prejudice and inner judgments we hold toward others. Only on such a path are we able to be truly present to each another. Only when we encounter others in an authentic manner are we allowed to trust that something is alive and stirring within them. But with Elizabeth we should desire to see Christ himself in each person we encounter on Christmas, including those in our own family. We should say with Elizabeth:

And why has this happened to me, that the mother of my Lord comes to me? (Lk. 1:43)

Only then are we able to experience the coming of Christmas as a feast of encounter and celebrate it as a feast of the family. But this also means that only then will we be able to encounter *ourselves* in a new manner.

❧ Practice

Imagine the individual members of your family, one by one. You know something about each of them. But go further, beyond what you already know about them. Each of them in an important sense remains a mystery to you. Each of them bears Christ in themselves, for Christ dwells in the innermost heart of each person.

Consider how in each of them—and in all people—a good kernel is to be found, for each contains an inner longing to be good. Each is a brother or sister of Jesus. Each holds within themselves an inner room where God himself dwells. Not even all the mistakes we might make can disturb this sacred center, for there each person is holy, unique, and original.

Think about each person in your family, one by one. Consider how you might encounter them as a way of discovering this truth, today and throughout the coming days. Think about how you might bow before each one, and later, when you speak with one or the other, think about how you might bow to them in the manner of your encounter. When you do this, you'll find yourself able to be present to them in a truly different manner than you might otherwise have.

December 24
CELEBRATING A NEW BEGINNING

THE GREAT SAINT of the fifth century Pope Leo the Great wrote of the truth of this season in a beautiful way:

> When we encounter the appearance of our savior in humility, we come to see clearly that we are celebrating our own beginnings. . . . Christian, recognize your own worth! You have come to share in the divine nature. Don't return to your old wretchedness, and don't live beneath your true worth.

At Christmas, we celebrate our true origins, coming to know that we are not held hostage by our past. Yes, we've made mistakes. We've hurt and been hurt by others. Many of us, though, seem to imagine that our injuries and mistakes prevent us from ever making a new beginning. But we know that within each of us is the longing to begin afresh, to leave the old self behind us and stop circling endlessly around our hurts or opportunities we squandered in the past. Today, on Christmas Eve, we come to realize that a new beginning is always possible, that it's never too late to start again. Christmas is the invitation to initiate a new beginning in our lives, and begin to live from things we might have long dreamed of but prevented ourselves from enjoying because of the ways we have undervalued ourselves.

On Christmas we celebrate our own true dignity. For God became a human being so that we humans might also become divine, each of us coming to share in the divine life. This reminds us that our origins are not merely finite and earthly. No, God descended into each of us in order to penetrate all that is human and earthly in us with his divine love and life.

When I notice my breath what I experience is not simply the movement of air. It is, rather, the divine Spirit I am inhaling. And in my breath God's Spirit, God's love, flows into and through me. I come to know that the divine life within me is not limited by death.

On Christmas we celebrate the good news that we carry within us something death cannot destroy, that we have an inner life which is divine and indestructible. This is what shows us our true worth, which doesn't depend on our achievements. Rather, it has to do with who we really are as children of God made in God's very image. Paul, addressing the philosophers in Athens, put it this way:

> For "in him we live and move and have our being"; as even some of your own poets have said. (Acts 17:28)

☙ Practice

Imagine how you were on the day of your birth: naked, and not yet completely formed. Your entire life still lay before you; no one had yet told you how you should live. In God's eyes, you were unspeakably free, the perfect image God had made for you. No conditions had yet been set for your life, and you were free of the expectations, wishes, and projections others might later come to have for you.

Imagine, then, that God sees your freedom *today* in the very same way. God does not want to bind you or hold you down. God desires this day to begin anew with you. For God is the one who is always eternally new. And when this God is born within you, everything becomes new in your life. You can shape your life anew and form your relationships in new ways. You find that you are freed of the burdens you carried in the past.

Thank God that he takes you by the hand this day and walks with you. Each step you take is one you make with him in this new way. And when you have become a new being, your relationships with others can be formed on a new basis, one that makes room for this new life to take shape and grow.

Afterword

Advent and Christmas are for many of us a favorite time of the year. During these weeks we find our hearts warmed by the stories and traditions we encounter, leading many among us to desire experiencing these seasons with greater intentionality. The reflections and practices I have gathered in this book are meant to meet this desire.

The Swiss psychoanalyst Carl Jung approached the entire church year as a therapeutic system, seeing each season of the year as a time of healing, because each one has to do with some inner aspect of the soul. He helped us see that the manner in which we grasp particular images—or what he called "archetypes"— can have a profoundly healing effect on us. They can bring us in touch with the soul's healing powers, accessing in their depths the things that help us by offering us what we need to grow in our lives. This soul-wisdom, however, is often obscured by the mass of information and images that inundate us and saturate our lives through the media.

I'd like to share some additional thoughts at the end of this book which point to healing images that come to us in Advent and at Christmas, opening us to experience the power of this season to heal our wounds and bring us in touch with the healing powers of the soul.

While each season of the church's year offers us a time of healing, this is above all true for Advent and Christmas. Why? Because it is during this period that we witness images held in our souls—Jung's archetypes again—that have slumbered within humankind for thousands of years. Part of the reason Christmas is so beloved among us is because of the way it brings these images to light in us. Many among us, of course, are no longer conscious of these images, but it often happens that something—a Christmas carol, the aroma of a freshly cut Christmas tree, the gentle light of candles, or the images we encounter at Christmas and in the nativity scenes we set out in our homes and churches— stirs these archetypes within us. When this happens, we find ourselves reminded of the images we carry deep in our hearts that the mystery of Advent and Christmas addresses in unique and powerful ways.

Transforming Addiction into Yearning

Throughout these meditations I have addressed the importance yearning plays in human experience. I realize that this language might be unfamiliar or uncomfortable for those who'd prefer not to speak of such things openly. Psychology has made us aware, though, that the addictions which trouble many of us are actually an expression of suppressed desire. For this reason, Advent is a time to experience how such addictive behavior might be transformed in our lives.

Recently, a therapist I know invited me to come speak at a conference on addiction, asking me to address how addiction might be transformed into yearning. For he knew, as I do, that addiction cannot be healed through discipline or relational psychology alone, even while such things are helpful for those who suffer from it. For transformation to occur, addiction must be healed at its root, not merely by treating its symptoms. This is where the question of suppressed desire comes into play.

One school of psychology sees addiction as a form of mother replacement. That is, at the hidden core of an addiction is our longing for a lost paradise—in this case, the sense of being held securely in our mother's womb. An alcoholic turns to drink to experience something of this feeling, while a drug addict seeks an experience of ecstasy in order to forget life's demands and troubles. A workaholic wishes to be esteemed and respected for what they achieve through their work, using their immersion in their work to avoid coming to terms with some truth about themselves they are unwilling or unable to face.

Those addicted to gambling desire to experience, by means of a stroke of good luck or great success, what it feels like to recover their lost sense of paradise. But the more they play, and the greater their bets become, the more they find themselves enslaved by their passions and desires in their hope to secure their happiness. On this path, however, they'll find themselves forever chasing an elusive goal that they can never finally reach.

The time of Advent with its flickering candles and wafts of the sweet aroma of evergreen branches instills within us a childlike sense of being held, a feeling of being-at-home (*Heimat*) that we first come to know as children but continue to long for as adults. But Advent is not merely some nostalgic yearning for the lost goodness of childhood. Rather, it brings us in touch with our desire for a true sense of inner comfort and well-being, something we knew as children and long to experience again, if in a different form. For we cannot simply return to a childhood untroubled by responsibilities. We need to find our way, as adults who are responsible for ourselves and others, back to our heart in order to experience a sense of true well-being, that feeling of being truly at home in ourselves. This, finally, is God.

According to Jung, we remain infantile throughout our lives if we presume to have finished as adults with this mother love. This confusion can lead us into real difficulties as we grow older. What we need are symbols that can take this yearning for our mother, and the life energy we invest in it, and transform it into a healing and life-affirming power in our lives. Of course, many among us cannot tolerate the tensions that exist between our yearnings and the lack of fulfillment we often experience. And no celebration of Christmas, however beautiful it might be, can fulfill our deepest desires. All that we do can only awaken our yearning for more love and a truer sense of home, but the sense of fulfillment we might attain through our efforts will remain bound by our limited human experience. God alone is able to fulfill our deepest desires, while an addiction tries to bridge the tension between our longings and our lack of fulfillment. That is, it tries to produce a sense of this longed-for fulfillment, but it does so deceptively. Only when we direct our desire to God are our yearnings able to help us grow, spurring us forward and bringing us inner peace.

Only when I focus my desires on God do I find myself better able to accept my life for what it is, which in its ordinariness makes me aware that I cannot simply fulfill my wishes on my own. Only when I come to recognize that nothing I do of myself—my work, the activities I engage in, or my relationships with others—can fulfill my deepest yearning do I find myself able to give myself to my work and to my love for my partner with true enjoyment. For then I'm truly able to receive what I've been given. And whatever I experience in terms of my desires I can accept and direct to God. This keeps me alive, and it gives me a sense of inner peace.

The Image of the Divine Child

Above all else Christmas has to do with two healing images: first, the image of the divine child waiting to be born within us; and, second, the image of a new beginning. Psychologists tell us that we carry both a wounded child and a divine child within us. What this means is that the wounded child tends to cry out whenever we've been hurt just as we'd done as children when we felt abandoned, ignored, ridiculed, or scolded. It still falls to us as men and women with fatherly and motherly responsibilities to embrace the wounded child we carry within us so that the crying lessens, until the point where the child finally finds rest.

But this does not mean we should become content with this wounded child; rather, our work is to grow into the "divine child" we also hold within us. This child is for us an image of a reality we can only speak of in images and metaphors; it represents the unique image God has of us, which is to say the primal and unspoiled image of God within us. When we find a way to come into contact with this image, we have the chance of becoming truly ourselves, and in this sense like the divine child we see lying in the manger. In such a way, we find ourselves able to let go of the images others might have of us, together with images we've cultivated ourselves that falsely belittle us or elevate us wrongly in our own eyes. In affirming the divine child within us we become who we truly are, and, in this sense, are truly free. We no longer need to justify ourselves, and can let go of the compulsion to show off or prove ourselves to others. We can simply be. This state of freedom finds eloquent expression in lines from the mystic and poet Angelus Silesius:

The rose lives without any why,
and blooms to be itself and free.
It pays no attention to what it is
and does not ask if others see.

Many healing images are conveyed by this notion of divine child, a symbol that points to the source of our creativity and imagination. When we come into contact with this child, we find ourselves coming alive inside, acquiring new ideas and a kind of radiance that lights up our demeanor. Even our way of speaking changes, since we no longer talk on and on about things of little importance, but rather give way to something deep within us that begins to speak. We cease talking about ourselves, and find a fresh desire to engage in our work, because we begin to discover new things that delight us.

Our awareness of the divine child is what makes it possible for us to withstand crises in our lives and handle the dangers that threaten our existence. This divine child shows us where we might find fountains of life to drink from in the deserts we face, leading us to comfort and security even in the face of an experience of abandonment. It supports us when we might otherwise feel ready to quit, giving us a sense that life is meaningful after all and that we can go on in the midst of the difficulties we face.

The image of the divine child also plays a prominent role in the mythology of ancient peoples as a renewing power within each human being. The Romans spoke of it as the *puer aeternus,* the "eternal child," representing the experience of God's bringing forth something new from the ruins of the old. Even the Bible conveys this image in the prophet Isaiah's description of a shoot springing forth from the stump of Jesse. Early Christians took this promise as a prophecy referring to Jesus, in that the "divine child" in the manger comes to embody this in human form:

A shoot shall come out from the stump of Jesse,
and a branch shall grow out of his roots. (Isa. 11:1)

The divine child offers in such varied portrayals an image of wholeness, one able to unite within us the tensions and contradictions of our lives. According to Jung, this child is "a symbol which unites the opposites, a mediator, a healer who is capable of making things whole [*Ganzmacher*]." The prophet Isaiah describes the purpose of this divine child through a marvelous image:

The wolf shall live with the lamb,
the leopard shall lie down with the kid,
the calf and the lion the fatling together,
and a little child shall lead them. . . .
The nursing child shall play over the hole of the asp,
and the weaned child shall put its hand on the adder's den.
(Isa. 11:6–8)

When this divine child is at work within us, the tensions we experience between aggression and love, spirituality and sexuality, power and weakness, man and woman, fall away. Everything becomes unified within us, and no one of these forces comes to have power over us. Our life becomes playful and free.

The Image of a New Beginning

Another healing image we celebrate at Christmas is that of a new beginning, for in this season we celebrate God's new beginning among us. The old things that once had power over us in adverse ways lose their grip. We find ourselves emboldened to dream new dreams filled with the radiance of what is new.

Everything becomes possible. We no longer need to accept the old as a burden we must carry, but find ourselves able to make a new beginning.

German has two words for this experience: "to start something" (*anfangen*) and "to begin" (*beginnen*), each of which points to its own horizon of experience: "to start" means to "take hold of something, take it up, take it into our hands"; thus, when we speak of God making a new beginning in the birth of his Son, we are speaking of how God takes us also into his hands in order to form us anew. To say that we "begin" something suggests taking our lives into our own hands in order to give it shape. We quit complaining that we can't do anything, perhaps because of the ways we feel our upbringing to have determined our lives. Now, we have in hand what we need to direct our lives differently, and we can take what we've been given and form it according to our intentions. This requires us to take initiative ourselves, and not simply wait for others to do something on our behalf.

When we speak of "beginning" something, in German, we mean what in English would be rendered as "cultivating," since the origins of that word have an agricultural association (i.e., *urbar machen*). What lies behind this word is the image of a field filled with briars and thorns. An ancient story in the monastic tradition tells of a young disciple who comes to a revered old monk, complaining that he could go no further on the thorny path of ascetic discipline. His old failings continued to rise up in his life, and he couldn't clear his path of the weeds of bad behaviors. After listening to his complaints for some time, the elderly monk told this story: "A father sent his son to work in the field in order to cultivate it [*urbar machen*] for planting. But the field was so large and so choked with weeds that the young man left his work aside and lay down to rest, hoping to sleep after giving up his intention to clear the field of thistles. When his father checked after a few days had passed to see how his son was progressing, he gave him this advice: 'Each day do only as much work in the field as your body allows.' The son followed this advice, and after a short time was able to cultivate the entire field properly."

We often face the task of beginning with trepidation, perhaps because we're under the impression that we can't accomplish what's set before us, and thus can't find the strength to begin. We resign ourselves to thinking that we have no hope of succeeding at the tasks we face. The more we put off getting started, the harder it is to begin. What we learn from the Christmas story is that God "cultivates" the fields of this world through the birth of his Son. Through this event God plants the seeds of divine love in our souls as well, desiring that these seeds yield fruit in our lives. But this depends in part on us, for we are the ones who must cultivate the "field" that is our soul so that "the new thing" God has planted in us might grow and blossom. For God is the one who makes a new beginning in our lives, leaving the work of cultivating this beginning to us so that this work might in time yield the fruit of a bountiful harvest.

This image of a new beginning is filled with healing associations. Many among us, though, have the impression that their lives are determined through their past, feeling bound by their upbringing and the wounds they've suffered. They suffer from the lack of love they received, and the rejection they might have experienced. And thus they become paralyzed by their own failures through poor decisions they made or opportunities missed. Many complain on and on as if they could never live well because of all that went wrong in the past. In so doing, they cut themselves off from life.

The mystery of Christmas, however, reminds us of this: "*You are not determined by your past. You can begin again today, because you already carry something entirely new within you: the divine child is present in your life and can bring you in touch with what is new and neither spoiled nor depleted in your soul. Trust the new life that is within you!*"

Healing Symbols in Advent and Christmas

The three healing themes of Advent, explored above, are central for me. This season, of course, offers many other images, all of which have a healing radiance. Let me mention several more here.

THE ADVENT WREATH

Let us begin with the Advent wreath. What is a wreath? Historically, it was the symbol of victory, marking great success at some task or plan. We might understand the Advent wreath as pointing to the yearning we hold for a good life. It is not, of course, insignificant that we bring out this wreath in Advent as a way of marking the beginning of the church year. The wreath conveys the hope of this celebration and the images and stories it brings us, leading us on our journey into healing and wholeness, which is the true source of happiness in our lives.

Another image related to this wreath is that God holds all the broken parts of our lives together, smoothing the rough corners and rounding the edges of our experiences. For we constantly face the fragility of life, fearing that things might fall apart, knowing that the pressure of so many different needs might tear our lives asunder. We often have the feeling of sitting in the midst of the ruins of our lives. In such times, this wreath can be a symbol of hope, reminding us that the broken things will be held together and become part of a larger whole. This wreath also represents community, awakening us to the hope that our ways of being together—especially in our families—might flourish, since this season promises to bind us into one, in profound ways.

Each of the four candles on this wreath also has a specific meaning. The first stands for our longing for unity. The second points to the polarities of our lives—such as woman and man, right and left, conscious and unconscious—since all such opposing tensions are to be illumined through the light of Jesus. The third suggests the three dimensions of our existence, since we are made of body, soul, and spirit, or, in the terminology of the Enneagram, stomach, heart, and head. And the fourth, finally, reminds us of the four primal elements of earth, wind, water, and fire, suggesting how our daily life with all its earthly dimensions is to be illumined and transformed through Christ's light.

CANDLES

During Advent we also light candles in our homes. This is an ancient symbol, for the church has long had a tradition of using candles in worship and—at least in the Roman Catholic, Orthodox, and Anglican traditions—to accompany the reading from the book of the Gospels. They are for us a symbol of Christ, who said:

> *I am the light of the world. Whoever follows me will never walk in darkness but will have the light of life. (John 8:12)*

Among the candles used in the church, the Christ Candle holds special importance, symbolizing the light of Christ chasing away the darkness of death. During Advent and Christmas, of course, this candle has another meaning: the flame, which draws on the wax for its fire, represents the incarnation of God in Jesus Christ, and the light transforms all that is earthly (i.e., the wax) into a bright light. This light is gentle, a light that doesn't render judgment but rather illumines and transforms all that is within us. In this particular sense, the candle can also be understood as a symbol of those who are saved, an image in which we find ourselves healed and made whole. For the light of Christ is what illumines us.

To sit before a lighted candle and meditate on its gentle light means something special for me: when I do this, I hold all that is within me, even that which I hide from others and often enough from myself—which is to say, my mistakes and weaknesses, my suppressed needs and addictions—and allow all of this to be illumined by the gentle light of Jesus. I often meditate in the presence of a candle on the words of the prophet Isaiah:

> *The people who walked in darkness*
> *have seen a great light;*
> *those who lived in a land of deep darkness—*
> *on them light has shined. (Isa. 9:2)*

When I do this, I find that the fear I harbor toward the darkness in my soul subsides, and so too my fear of the darkness in the world around me. When I gaze into the flame of the candle, I find myself strengthened to trust that everything I carry within me will be illumined, that the light of Christ will enlighten my own soul, and that the ground of my soul is nothing other than light itself.

THE CHRISTMAS TREE

Even though the Christmas tree did not became widespread as a tradition in Germany until the nineteenth century, its symbolic value goes deep. On the one hand, it stands for Christ as the true tree of life, since the tree itself is a sign of the joining of heaven and earth, just as we say that the birth of Jesus joins the earthly and heavenly in one. The evergreen tree also represents our participation in the undying life of God, pointing as well to the two trees in paradise, namely, the tree of life and the tree of the knowledge of good and evil.

In Christ, we receive the fullness of life, for he gives us back a measure of the original life humans knew in paradise. As a symbol for the tree of knowledge, whose fruits Adam and Eve ate, people have long hung apples on their Christmas trees; thus, while Adam and Eve were forced from paradise because of their disobedience, so we believe that Christ's obedience restores us to the knowledge of God, that through him we're assured that we will not be expelled again from paradise. Wherever Christ dwells is for us the garden of paradise.

Another tradition is to decorate this tree with balls, since the ball is a symbol of eternal life, of all that is complete and unites opposing tensions in one. Thus, in Christ we believe that earth and heaven, light and darkness, God and humanity are joined to each other. Even if we think of the Christmas tree primarily in terms of its decorations, it can still stand as a healing symbol for us, for it comes to represent for us both the mystery of Jesus's birth and the mystery of our own lives as we are to be transformed through this birth.

THE MANGER

The manger is an important Christmas symbol, first popularized by St. Francis of Assisi in the thirteenth century. He inaugurated the very first outdoor Christmas celebration in the Italian town of Greccio, placing the manger at the very center of a "live" nativity and surrounding it with the figures found in the story of Jesus's birth. His intent was to engage all our senses through a simple portrayal of this story. And while this enactment was eventually forbidden by Protestant churches during the Reformation period, the Roman Catholic renewal of the later sixteenth and seventeenth centuries afforded the nativity a central place in the home, where it came to have special prominence in family life. Since that time, it is traditional for families to build their own, often quite elaborate nativity sets, using figures that may have been handed down through the family for generations—Mary and Joseph, the baby Jesus, the shepherds and angels, and of course later, the three kings.

The nativity set not only recalls Jesus's birth once long ago in a manger in Bethlehem but also offers us an image of our own lives. We should become a "manger" in which Jesus might be born again. We do this by offering our poor and humble hearts to Jesus, with all the ordinariness that is within us together with all that is untidy, unclean, and earthly in our hearts. The manger shows us even more than this: our wretchedness and, at the same time, the transformation of the manger through the divine child. Artists through the ages have presented this child as radiant with light, for it is Christ who brings light to my poverty, into the manger that is my life in all its daily dimensions. Christ transforms my life!

THE ANGELS

No Christmas celebration is complete without angels. Both Luke and Matthew tell us of their role in announcing to both Mary and Joseph the tidings of Jesus's birth. Luke presents us with the Christmas angel who brings the message of the Messiah's birth to the shepherds, an angel he portrays as shining with divine radiance. He brings light into the dark night of these shepherds, and joy to them in their desolation:

Do not be afraid; for see—I am bringing you good news of great joy for all the people. (Lk. 2:10)

Added to this is the image of "a multitude of the heavenly host" of angels (Lk. 2:13), praising God with songs inspired by Christmas:

Glory to God in the highest heaven,
and on earth peace among those whom he favors. (Lk. 2:14)

Artists have favored these angels above all others in their artwork, presenting them in delightful ways. Often they're portrayed as small, childlike angels, singing their hearts out in the heavenly choir, often playing instruments to accompany their song. These angels usually have wings, a sign both of their bridging of heaven and earth and of the lightness of being they bring to our lives. They seem to desire to give wings to our souls, reminding us not to take ourselves so seriously or approach our lives in such ponderous ways. They want to sing Christmas joy into our hearts.

When we look at the angels we see in Christmas paintings, we find our hearts lightened within us. They remind us of all that is light, joyful, and bright in our souls. They bring us in touch with our longing for joy, fulfillment, light, and joyful music. Angels are God's messengers sent into our nights to bring light into the darkness we experience, meeting us in our fears in order to transform them into trust and joy. They are ambassadors for God, reminding us that the Lord desires to dwell within us. In all such ways we should look for the manger with its singing angels within our lives. We need such angels in order to discover in new ways the riches of our souls at Christmas. They represent the potential of our souls, standing for all the possibilities and resources God has placed in our hearts, gifts we often ignore or obscure through our worries and fears. Thus it is good for us to pay attention to these angels as they have been so tenderly painted and sculpted over the centuries.

THE STAR

A further Advent symbol is the star. Matthew reports that a star rose in the east, drawing the three Magi to journey toward Bethlehem from the orient, for they interpreted this as a sign that a royal child would be born in Judea. The star guided them from afar to the manger, but it is not confined to this story of the Wise Men. It reminds us also of the symbolic power stars have as lights in the dark night sky, representing the radiance that penetrates and transforms the darkness we must face. There is a Jewish tradition which claims that every star has a guardian angel, since they show us a way through the darkness of our lives like angels accompanying us on our way.

The Latin word for desire, *desiderium*, holds within it the word for star (*sidera*). Our desires were thus understood to bring the stars to the earth, and for this reason stars have often been associated with our yearnings. Often, this has to do with our longing for home or for love. When we find ourselves in an unknown place, and gaze at the heavens at night, we can imagine that the very same heavens show their radiance to those we love who are far away. The stars bind us with the ones we cherish, and often enough it seems that the heavens are the only connection we have when we are far from home. Just so, when we see an image of the Christmas star we find ourselves reminded of how we are bound with our heavenly home, for we are not simply "home" in the place where we grew up. As the apostle Paul put it:

Our citizenship is in heaven. (Phil. 3:20)

THE CELEBRATION OF CHRISTMAS

When you and your family shape the Advent season on the basis of the meditations and practices I have suggested in this book, Christmas will become for you a truly consecrated season. It will become a celebration above all others in which you find yourself able to feel God's birth in your life. And it will become a family festival in which you find yourselves enabled to encounter each other in new and life-giving ways. It will become a feast celebrating a new beginning in your lives.

We know, of course, that a festival needs preparation. One cannot simply leave the hectic pace of life behind and somehow burst into the Christmas celebration without properly preparing for the coming of this gift. For if our hearts are not quiet within us, we have little hope of celebrating Christmas as the joyous celebration it is meant to be. In such a case, of course, we should not expect to experience our family as a place of healing and wholeness. And we must admit that preparations alone are no guarantee that we'll truly enjoy such a celebration, though they do open us to the mystery of this wondrous season and make us more conscious and attentive to its wonders.

The Italian word for Christmas is *natale*, referring to the birth of Jesus we celebrate in this season, while the English *Christmas* points to the church's worship, or the "Mass" when we celebrate Christ's birth. In German, we have a quite different word: *Weihnachten*, which reminds us that this is a consecrated night (from the verb *weihen*, which means "to make holy"), a night that is itself "made holy" through Jesus's birth. Holiness is what was taken from the world, and thus when we speak of *Weihnachten* we are pointing to the hope that all that is dark in this night, and in our lives, might be illumined with the light of Christ. It is our fervent desire that our spiritual "night," with all its depressions and sorrows, might be transformed into a consecrated night, a night "made holy" through this birth. On this special night, we find ourselves encouraged in our hope that the God who is born in Jesus will come to us to heal our wounds. For since antiquity people believed that only a holy one could heal as a sign of being "made holy." But the holy needs a special way of engaging us, namely, our readiness to be affected and touched by the divine, to encounter it fully in our humility.

When we celebrate this holy night, this *Weihnacht*, with humility, we find that the holy words we hear in these stories begin to speak to us in new ways. When my own father read the Christmas story from Luke's Gospel on Christmas Eve as we children gathered in front of the Christmas tree, I experienced something of this holiness. We listened attentively as he read these words:

> *To you is born this day in the city of David a Savior, who is the Messiah, the Lord. (Lk. 2:11)*

When we heard these words read, we sensed something of their holiness. They moved us in our hearts. What a good reminder that Christmas is something more than a celebration of tasty food. It needs the presence of the holy so that it might become a healing celebration for each of us and for our families.

When I think of Christmas, the words of the apostle Paul in his letter to Titus come particularly to mind:

> *But when the goodness and loving kindness of God our Savior appeared, he saved us. (Titus 3:4)*

Peter Wust, a Catholic philosopher who died in 1940, sent his friends a letter of parting shortly before his early death to cancer. In it he quoted these words in Latin: *benignitas et humanitas Dei salvatoris nostri.* During the last years of his later life, when Germany was ruled by the Nazis, this claim sounded a courageous and hopeful message: against the inhumanity and hatefulness of this dictatorship, Jesus represented our *humanitas*, our "humanity," and God's "benignity" toward all human beings offered us an image of what humanity truly entails. These are thus holy and healing words, for through the coming of Jesus Christ the world became holier, brighter, and more human.

Another holy word that we hear read during the Christmas celebration of worship is the message found in John's Gospel, a Christmas story of a quite different dimension:

> *And the Word became flesh and lived among us, and we have seen his glory, the glory as of a father's only son, full of grace and truth. (John 1:14)*

One cannot explain these words. One can only encounter them in wonder. For the mystery we proclaim is that the divine Word became flesh in a little child lying in a manger, taking vulnerable human form so that we might be enabled to see God's beauty in the humanity of this Son. And this is a beauty "full of grace," as John puts it, which is to say, one who is full of loveliness and tenderness.

It is a beauty that stirs us and fills us with love and gratitude. But it is also a beauty "full of truth," one that reveals to us the presence of what it means to be truly human. If for the Greeks truth suggested a kind of veil draped over all that is, this veil has been lifted away for us, allowing us to gaze upon the ground of being itself.

In this child in the manger we see the true form of humanity. In him, the truth of God comes to illumine our lives. In him, God reveals God's very self to us, disclosing this gift to us in order to show himself to us, veiled in human form. In the pure face of this child we come to see the very face of God.

My prayer for you is that you might recognize the beauty of God in this Advent and Christmas season—in the child lying in the manger and in all the paintings made through the centuries, each of which reveals something of this story to us. Each conveys a measure of the profound mystery this celebration holds and reveals, pointing to the goodness and kindness of God toward us and all humanity. As you come to sense more and more of this divine beauty, I hope you might discover its radiance in your own face, and sense it in the faces of those around you.

My wish for you is that the holy words we hear in Advent and at Christmas might bring healing to you, that the sacred season of Christmas might heal your wounds. I pray that you might experience the divine child in your life, the child who brings you in touch with your true self.

And I encourage you to remember that this divine child is to be found in everyone you encounter. May many of the experiences you'll have during Advent and Christmas remind you of the holiness you carry within yourself, and of that which is waiting to be found in everyone you know and all those you'll meet. Insofar as you experience this, your encounters will be saving ones, bringing the experience of healing and bringing a blessing to you and those around you. I pray that this Christmas blessing will flow through you and, in this way, help transform the world into a place of peace, a place in which you experience something of the true "home" that God's loving nearness promises.

ABOUT PARACLETE PRESS

Who We Are

Paraclete Press is a publisher of books, recordings, and DVDs on Christian spirituality. Our publishing represents a full expression of Christian belief and practice—from Catholic to Evangelical, from Protestant to Orthodox.

We are the publishing arm of the Community of Jesus, an ecumenical monastic community in the Benedictine tradition. As such, we are uniquely positioned in the marketplace without connection to a large corporation and with informal relationships to many branches and denominations of faith.

What We Are Doing

PARACLETE PRESS BOOKS | Paraclete publishes books that show the richness and depth of what it means to be Christian. Although Benedictine spirituality is at the heart of all that we do, we publish books that reflect the Christian experience across many cultures, time periods, and houses of worship. We publish books that nourish the vibrant life of the church and its people.

We have several different series, including the bestselling Paraclete Essentials and Paraclete Giants series of classic texts in contemporary English; Voices from the Monastery—men and women monastics writing about living a spiritual life today; award-winning poetry; bestselling gift books for children on the occasions of baptism and first communion; and the Active Prayer Series that brings creativity and liveliness to any life of prayer.

MOUNT TABOR BOOKS | Paraclete's newest series, Mount Tabor Books, focuses on the arts and literature as well as liturgical worship and spirituality, and was created in conjunction with the Mount Tabor Ecumenical Centre for Art and Spirituality in Barga, Italy.

PARACLETE RECORDINGS | From Gregorian chant to contemporary American choral works, our recordings celebrate the best of sacred choral music composed through the centuries that create a space for heaven and earth to intersect. Paraclete Recordings is the record label representing the internationally acclaimed choir Gloriæ Dei Cantores, praised for their "rapt and fathomless spiritual intensity" by *American Record Guide*; the Gloriæ Dei Cantores Schola, specializing in the study and performance of Gregorian chant; and the other instrumental artists of the Arts Empowering Life Foundation.

Paraclete Press is also privileged to be the exclusive North American distributor of the recordings of the Monastic Choir of St. Peter's Abbey in Solesmes, France, long considered to be a leading authority on Gregorian chant.

PARACLETE VIDEO | Our DVDs offer spiritual help, healing, and biblical guidance for a broad range of life issues including grief and loss, marriage, forgiveness, facing death, bullying, addictions, Alzheimer's, and spiritual formation.

Learn more about us at our website:
www.paracletepress.com or phone us
toll-free at 1.800.451.5006

SCAN
TO
READ
MORE

All Creation Waits:
The Advent Mystery of New Beginnings

GAYLE BOSS

978-1-61261-785-5 | $18.99 Paperback – Fully illustrated

Open a window each day of Advent onto the natural world. Here are twenty-five fresh images of the foundational truth that lies beneath and within the Christ story. In twenty-five portraits depicting how wild animals of North America ingeniously adapt when darkness and cold descend, we see and hear as if for the first time the ancient wisdom of Advent: The dark is not an end but the way a new beginning comes.

Short, daily reflections that paint vivid, poetic images of familiar animals, paired with charming original wood-cuts, will engage both children and adults. Anyone who does not want to be caught, again, in the consumer hype of "the holiday season" but rather to be taken up into the eternal truth the natural world reveals will welcome this book.

"Each of the beautiful creatures in this little book is a unique word of God, its own metaphor, all of them together drawing us to the One we all belong to."

—Richard Rohr, OFM

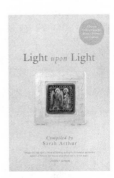

Light Upon Light:
A Literary Guide to Prayer for Advent, Christmas, and Epiphany

SARAH ARTHUR

978-1-61261-419-9 | $18.99 Paperback

This collection of daily and weekly readings goes through the liturgical seasons of winter—including Advent, Christmas, and Epiphany. New voices such as Amit Majmudar and Scott Cairns are paired with well-loved classics by Dickens, Andersen, and Eliot.

"For years I have been seeking a book which weaves scripture, prayer and the finest poetry and fiction into the devotional experience of Advent, Christmas, and Epiphany. Finally I have found it: an elegant and accessible gem with some classic texts and a rich selection from contemporary literature. This is not only a useful book, it is edifying and exciting reading—the perfect way for the literature lover to focus, meditate, and celebrate this time of year."

—Jill Peláez Baumgaertner, poet; Professor of English and Dean of Humanities and Theological Studies, Wheaton College